PORTFOLIO
# BHUJIA BARONS

Pavitra Kumar was born in Deolali, Maharashtra, in 1985. An army officer's daughter, she travelled across India from a young age and developed a keen appreciation of people and places. She completed her undergraduate degree in journalism from Delhi University in 2003 before a short stint with CNN-IBN in Delhi. In 2006, Pavitra went to London to pursue a career in marketing and worked for digital marketing agencies in management roles, spending much of her time liaising with the press and writing professional articles representing her firm. At the same time, her love for writing pushed her to freelance with the-nri.com. She completed her MBA from the Carlson Institute of Management in May 2016, and continues to pursue her love for business and passion for writing.

Pavitra lives in Lakeville, Minnesota, with her husband, Dr Aditya Raghunathan, and mini goldendoodle, Lily. Trekking, swimming, reading and coffee keep her going when she isn't writing.

# PAVITRA KUMAR

# BHUJIA BARONS

## THE UNTOLD STORY OF HOW
# HALDIRAM
## BUILT A ₹5000-CRORE EMPIRE

PORTFOLIO
PENGUIN

An imprint of Penguin Random House

PORTFOLIO

USA | Canada | UK | Ireland | Australia
New Zealand | India | South Africa | China

Portfolio is part of the Penguin Random House group of companies
whose addresses can be found at global.penguinrandomhouse.com

Published by Penguin Random House India Pvt. Ltd
7th Floor, Infinity Tower C, DLF Cyber City,
Gurgaon 122 002, Haryana, India

Penguin
Random House
India

First published in Portfolio by Penguin Random House India 2016

ISBN 9788184007558

Typeset in Adobe Jenson Pro by Manipal Digital Systems, Manipal
Printed at Replika Press Pvt. Ltd, India

# CONTENTS

*Prologue*                                          xi

*Introduction*                                      xvii

PART I
Haldiram                                            1

PART II
Greener Pastures                                    39

PART III
The Capital                                         77

PART IV
The Black Sheep                                     123

PART V
Legal Entanglements                                 177

PART VI
Final Paces                                         199

*Acknowledgements*                                  221

# THE AGARWALS

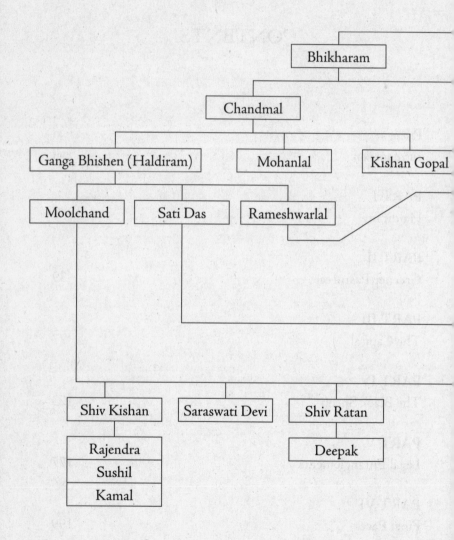

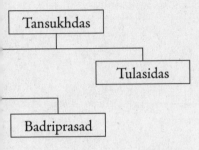

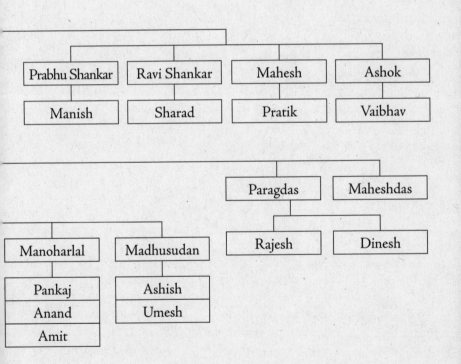

# BHUJIA BARONS

# PROLOGUE

## Fire, Ashes and a Phoenix Rises

### 31 October 1984

It was just another ordinary Wednesday afternoon. The market was bustling with tourists, students, housewives and merchants—all in throes of besting shopkeepers for the cheapest deals they could find. The merchants, in turn, worked their charm in frenzy, moving their arms around animatedly, calling out their meanest deals, 'Three for ₹10! Three for ₹10!' while arrogantly boasting about the 'highest quality' products!

The narrow streets were packed with people, animals, cycles, autorickshaws and Bajaj scooters. It was a wonder that so much could thrive and exist in those tapered lanes of Chandni Chowk. Dust, soot and the bright harsh sunlight of the afternoon did nothing to deter the daily mission. Beggars unabashedly grabbed any limbs within reach, hoping to wheedle a few paise out of passers-by, and thieves quietly pocketed errant knick-knacks hoping to disappear unnoticed into the anonymity of the crowd.

In the midst of this chaos, groups of people gathered around radios in local teashops, cheering India's cricket team in a very intense one-day international against Pakistan in Sialkot. Dilip Vengsarkar was in his element and close to scoring a century against India's bitterest rivals in cricket. He endeared himself to the crowd even more when he hit another four, forcing the Pakistani fielders to sprint across the field in vain. The audience in Chandni Chowk roared in delight as the announcer on All India Radio described this young player's incredible performance. There was cheering and excitement all around. Everyone was a stranger in those small groups around the radio, yet they hugged and shook hands as if they were brothers.

The warm camaraderie was the hallmark of Chandni Chowk. This crowded district, where one could barely walk without brushing against vibrant life, was an amalgamation of religious harmony. Between the Jama Masjid, Gurdwara Sis Ganj Sahib and the Digambara Jain temple, people of all religious identities and walks of life had lived there in congruence and peace for centuries. All of which was about to come to a brutal end on this very ordinary Wednesday.

The enthusiastic group listening intently to the match on the radio was sorely disappointed when the game was interrupted by an announcement on All India Radio. It declared that the BBC had said that Prime Minister Indira Gandhi had been assassinated earlier that morning. Confused and alarmed, the group huddled closer together. Gradually, the teashops became the centre points where everyone wanted to be. People gathered, straining to listen so they could catch more details, hardly believing their ears.

At six that evening, the vice president of India, R. Venkataraman, announced that Rajiv Gandhi had been sworn in as prime minister following Indira Gandhi's death earlier that day. Slowly, the grim confirmation spread like a virus, alerting everybody that two Sikh soldiers had shot down the prime minister. Through the noise and chaos, people received intelligence of outbreaks of violence near the All India Institute of Medical Sciences. Finally, that evening, a curfew was declared asking all shopkeepers to shut shop and all citizens to stay indoors until the government deemed it safe to be out on the streets again.

Multiple whisperings and mutterings later, the crowded market had finally quieted down, as every shop was shuttered and people retired for the night.

A young Marwari businessman, who had just opened a snack shop in the Katara Lachchu Singh area of Chandni Chowk a year ago, welcomed a night of respite after months of hard work. He hoped to get back to work in the morning, fresh and feisty after the curfew was lifted. The businessman and his large joint family lived on a lane adjacent to the Gurdwara Sis Ganj Sahib above a Sikh baker's shop. His wife and kids and brother's family had all reached home by the time Manoharlal got home, settling down for a family meal on the floor of their tiny, cramped living room. It had taken months of cajoling his father and grandfather to move to Delhi and then endless eighteen-hour workdays to set up their small eight-by-eleven-foot shop in Chandni Chowk. Manoharlal was proud of his achievement and felt thankful to be living in the Rajdhani, his heart filled with the hope of economic promise.

Unbeknownst to this peaceful sleeping family, a throng was growing in strength and unruliness that night. Cries of 'blood for blood' echoed into the dark, as they grew more aggressive. The cries quickly turned to action as the mobs began to ransack houses and shops in the middle of the night and cut down unsuspecting victims with knives and farmers' sickles.

On 1 November 1984, Manoharlal and his family woke up hoping to hear something positive on the radio, but were instead greeted with news that dangerous mobs were roaming the city with a singular chant of 'kill the sardars!' The jovial family felt an eerie unease. Even the two-year-old Ashish Agarwal became unusually quiet, as though he knew something unholy was happening in the capital.

They could hear distant yells of carnage as they huddled together in their tiny apartment with a fervent prayer on their lips for all those on the street.

The Gurdwara Sis Ganj Sahib nearby was being sullied by angry mobs that pelted it with stones in the hopes of getting their violent hands on the Sikhs taking refuge inside. The gurdwara, one of the nine historical gurdwaras in Delhi, having faced much violence in the past, was standing strong once again for its people. Though the popular belief was that Chandni Chowk had always been a place of religious harmony, hundreds of years ago, in 1675 AD, Mughal emperor Aurangzeb had beheaded Guru Tegh Bahadur in the hallowed square in front of this very gurdwara for refusing to convert to Islam. A few brave Sikhs had then rallied around their sacred ground and kept it unsullied.

On that fateful day in 1984, however, aside from a few brave Hindu neighbours, there were no angels that came to protect the Sikhs. The square outside the gurdwara was wet with their blood, and in spite of the passage of several years and the trampling of thousands of feet, those stains of injustice have been barely rubbed off even to this day.

Manoharlal and his family felt fear for the community and their Sikh friends all around, but not for one moment did they believe that they would have as much to lose on that day.

There was insanity and an animal-like vengeance in the eyes of the perpetrators. The mobs were armed with iron rods and knives, kerosene and matches. Manoharlal could see distant flare of fire through the blinds in their apartment and felt his heart cringe at the inhumanity of these vulgar actions. Suddenly, a lick of flame flared too close to home. The family heard a lot of shouting and yelling and the apartment began to feel hotter. There were urgent bangs on the doors downstairs and he took charge, instantly leading his family out of the door. Something felt terribly wrong. They were all in their nightwear when they dashed down the stairs on to the streets, grabbing only their young ones. Material possessions felt immaterial in that moment.

It was lucky that he took that decision. Standing on the street, the family saw a part of their building blow up in an explosion of flames as the fire spread from the bakery below. Gas cylinders and cans of ghee added to the fireworks. The family watched their life's savings go up in flames and their future reduced to ashes.

Manohar felt his breath catch in his throat as he fought the waves of nausea that threatened to engulf him. Everything he had ever worked for, everything he had ever saved up, was right there, in those two small floors above the baker's shop. His security and the future of his children were fast evaporating into a dark and sooty sky. Holding his wife's and son's hands in his own, looking into his brother's eyes, he felt a growing determination. He would not give his father or grandfather the pleasure of saying, 'You should have listened to me.' He silently vowed not to accept defeat but to rise again like a phoenix from the ashes.

# INTRODUCTION

'Never be afraid to do something new.
Remember, amateurs built the ark; professionals
built the *Titanic*.'

—Anonymous

## Behemoths of Bikaner

Since time immemorial, snacks and sweets have been integral to Indian culture. Hundreds and thousands of hawkers and small shopkeepers have sold fried, savoury snacks and sweets made from ghee in paper cones to children and adults alike in bazaars and street corners for as far back as history can take us. This is the story of one such family from a small town in Rajasthan that revolutionized the snack food industry through original and ancient recipes as well as innovative selling and marketing techniques.

The Haldiram family business started when the patriarch Haldiram began making and selling a new snack—the *bhujia* we all know and love—to the locals in Bikaner in 1918. This family business has survived almost a hundred years of change and challenge to become one of India's most-loved packaged food brands today. Generations of the Haldiram family have stood by the family brand, each in their own way contributing to its growth, fame and notoriety. As with most family businesses, this too has seen its fair share of divisions over the years. The brand name is currently used by three completely independent businesses run by Haldiram's grandsons, namely Haldiram's Nagpur in Nagpur; Haldiram Bhujiawala, Haldiram's Prabhuji and Haldiram in Kolkata; and the best-known Haldiram's in Delhi.

The Haldiram Agarwals are a bunch of very private men who hold their loved ones close to their hearts, and their secrets, closer still. Potbellies, short physiques and twinkling eyes are not their only common features; they also share an identical, deeply ingrained drive to succeed—an ambition that has spanned a hundred years leading to this era where Haldiram is a name almost every Indian recognizes. These men rule their business empires with benevolence, humility and originality, while tightly holding the reins of all operations.

These Agarwals share a deep love for their business and products, and an even greater desire to leave behind a legacy, an impact on the world through the work they do. Nurtured by the traditional customs of Marwari culture, challenged by the disruption of modern technology and practices, they have continued to thrive to make Haldiram in all its names and forms a strong national and international player.

Visionaries, they share a common desire to learn from their mistakes and stay one step ahead of the future. They have achieved this near-impossible feat multiple times, surprising the market with simple yet ingenious solutions to problems that nobody even knew existed. In their fearlessness, they have grasped ideas both good and bad, and taken a leap of faith—faith in themselves and their abilities—to set in motion huge tidal waves of change.

It takes immense courage, creativity and sheer determination to rise from the dust in a small town in Rajasthan and become a brand that resonates with customers across the globe. Success never comes easy and this family has faced Herculean challenges in both their personal lives and in business to make it this far.

'It's a fantastic achievement,' said Anmol Dar, chairman of Superbrands Council India, to *Business Standard*, 'for a brand that literally grew from nowhere, to have consistently struck the right chord with customers. Also, Haldiram is one of the most recognized Indian brands internationally.'

Their innate understanding of the customer's tastes, wants and aspirations, even at a time when surveys or focus groups were uncommon, helped them consistently fulfil desires and build an almost cult-like loyal following. This, along with their keen business sense, perhaps a genetic boon from their Marwari ancestry, or retrospective wisdom through experience, or possibly pure luck, have them firmly rooted as India's most-loved snacks and sweets brand.

They are proud of their business achievements and eager to greet the future with more successes. However, they are also deeply devoted to their families. The distinction between a business decision and a familial one often blurs as they struggle to tread lightly on the razor edge of the tightrope between the two.

Their successes have come at a price, and while they certainly enjoy their place in the sun, they too have had many a dark moment. Like Mario Puzo very aptly noted in *The Godfather*, 'Every family has bad memories,' this family certainly has a few old cupboards filled with pain, endurance, loss and disappointment. It is these very moments that test the mettle of a man and define character. It is also these moments that have shaped the history of this empire and differentiated one brother from another.

They share the same genes, the same heritage and the same passion for bhujia, yet every day they strive to be different from one another and shine brighter in their own individual light. Possessive and territorial in a market where together they are leaders, they combat each other in a twenty-five-year-old battle in the courts of Delhi and Kolkata to carve out the bigger piece of their heritage for themselves. This is a complex family with many factions and loyalties, where at times blood and brotherhood are not synonymous.

With tough competition on the horizon, a changing modern customer, modern operational issues, attacks on their brand from the US Food and Drug Administration, accusations of attempted murder and constant familial strife—these men have faced many tough trials that will lay the foundations for the next few chapters of not only their own history, but also the history of the Indian snack food industry.

From their early start in the dusty streets of Bikaner, the adventurous foray into Bengal, Nagpur and Delhi, to the firm launch pad of international expansion, their struggle continued as they fought to define their brand inside the gritty walls of courthouses. This, then, is a story of these ordinary men who have achieved extraordinary feats.

# PART I

# HALDIRAM

# A Glimpse into the Future

On a hot summer afternoon in June 2015, after attending a half-day staff meeting with his procurement manager on the restaurant floor, the thirty-eight-year-old director, Pankaj Agarwal, was exhausted. He sat all alone in the white-walled boardroom furnished in rose wood in his Gurgaon office, with nothing but the low hum of the air conditioner to keep him company. The young heir to the Haldiram's empire in Delhi had just been rewarded for his hard work with incremental responsibilities. There was a lot resting on his shoulders and he had been given the opportunity he had been preparing for all his life. Yet, he was nervous, his exhausted mind confused and his palms sweaty.

Taking a deep breath, he tugged his tie loose and gracefully moved away from the table. 'Let your senses guide you,' Pankaj muttered to himself and opened the door of the boardroom to one of the familiar corridors of the office building. Picking up his pace, he walked briskly, almost with purpose, coming to a halt in front of an old, non-descript solid wooden door. Punching the code into the keypad on the side, he opened the door and stepped in.

Almost instantly, Pankaj felt his muscles relax and his neurons fire. He was home. He had felt special stepping into a room just like this one for the first time when he was a young man and had continued to feel special every single time he entered thereafter.

It was in a spice kitchen very similar to this room that he had been handed the magical key to success. Rather, this was where the magical key to success had been honed within him and nurtured for years. It is based on the secrets of a room like this one that a small family-owned business had become the nation's largest and most successful processed foods corporation—Haldiram's, his family's business.

He had started mixing, testing and tasting spices while still in college. It was almost second nature to him. 'Let your senses guide you,' is what his father had said to him the first time, and his father before him. Rolling up his sleeves, Pankaj went about collecting spices and some plain bhujia and settled himself at the mixing table, letting his thoughts wander. He had been given the responsibility to evaluate the merits of the company's growth plans from expansion to London to initiating offshoot brands into other spaces such as the food delivery market. Ambitious like the other Agarwals before him, Pankaj was eager to help the business grow. While territorial expansion was a key to growth, their history of brand struggles with other Haldiram outfits in Kolkata and the strength of their internal capabilities worried him. He began weighing the pros and cons of several future ventures such as diversifying product lines, establishing factories on foreign soil and experimenting with new channels and platforms such as the Internet for distribution.

The company had journeyed a long way from being a small local *namkeen* shop in Bikaner to having over 20 per cent market share in the packaged snacks and sweets business in India in 2014.[1] It was also one of India's most well-known brands abroad.

Mixing a little saffron with chillies, he realized the quality he admired the most about his grandfather, Haldiram—the ability to go forth into the darkness with an idea that had never been tried before. They had taken a local snack and turned it into a national craving by focusing on packaging and branding even before their countrymen had heard of the concepts.

Haldiram, along with his sons and grandsons, had bravely tried what had never been tested before. Indians as consumers were only attracted to fresh products. At a time when bhujia's shelf life was hardly one week, the company had ventured into the unknown, taken a risk and developed a product with an extended shelf life of six months just so they could reach customers across India and give them a taste of bhujia.

Pankaj wondered what an exciting time it must have been to enter the market with such a different product and convince retailers and distributors alike to give them trial shelf space. 'And look how far we've come,' he thought to himself. The strength of this business lies within its many relationships and ties with distributors and resellers. Haldiram's is now sold in almost all Indian grocery stores and supermarkets, as toppings for chaats in restaurants, its mithai sold as frozen goods abroad. It even sells especially small sachets that cost ₹5 and ₹10 at roadside kiosks. So much so that Haldiram's sachets are often used in place of currency when shopkeepers don't have small change!

The brand has survived the test of time. It stood tall when food giants such as Pepsi entered the Indian processed

---

[1] Haldiram Foods International Limited in Packaged Foods (India), Passport, Euromonitor International 2014.

food space with Lehar. It fought back and fought hard when superbrands like McDonald's entered the market with fast food. Instead of pandering to the modern, evolving consumer tastes towards pizzas and burgers, Haldiram's went deeper to their roots and differentiated itself by opening a chain of fast-food restaurants serving India's favourite snack-time delicacies. They had mouth-watering goodies from the east, west, south and north to indulge the varying fancies of every family member.

Learning from their global competitors rather than arrogantly shunning their positives, Haldiram's continued to inculcate success factors such as larger restaurants that seated over five hundred customers, had greater parking space and friendly local staff. From personal challenges to environmental, Haldiram's had withstood the punches and over the years come out even more successful—just like Rocky!

Time and again, they faced challenges. In 2015, Haldiram's in Delhi had a turnover of ₹2480 crore, or approximately $350 million—all this from working in the north Indian states as well as exporting their products to over twenty countries internationally. While growth was still steady, it was becoming harder and harder to push growth rates with these geographical restrictions. The company, over the decades, had tried innovative avenues to expand their business. They had expanded product lines from simple snacks to sweets, frozen foods and baked goods. They had successfully entered the quick service restaurants (QSR) space, earning revenues that surpassed those of McDonald's and Domino's[2] in India. However, in order to

---

[2] http://food.ndtv.com/food-drinks/haldirams-revenue-more-than-mcdonalds-and-dominos-combined-736975.

continue to grow, they needed to explore other avenues such as international expansion, extensions of product lines, mergers and acquisitions.

It was going to be a long haul and Pankaj needed to devise sound strategies to ensure future success for the Haldiram's family. What could he learn from the successes and failures of the past? What could he do differently? Where did the answer lie?

He wondered what his grandfather, Haldiram, would do. Would he throw caution to the wind and take emboldened steps or would he inch towards success slowly and in a calculated manner?

## The First Little Sapling

Stepping off the last rungs of the Bikaner Express at the Bikaner Junction railway station is akin to time travel. A swirling mist of dust immediately welcomes you and everything around takes on charming medieval sepia tones. The station itself has pale-pink architecture similar to those of havelis, with tiny, carved arches on the walls. The bright blue sky compliments and contrasts the pink architecture.

The drive from the station to Bhujia Bazaar is about three quarters of an hour and takes on a leisurely quality that one begins to subconsciously associate with this dusty, beautiful city. Despite heavy traffic comprised of motorbikes, autorickshaws, scooters and big trucks that have neatly painted messages such as 'horn please' or 'use dipper at night' inscribed on them, in the backdrop of myriad gently undulating sand dunes, Bikaner presents a surreal, other-worldly charm.

The city has seen a glorious past with the lavish lives of virtuous maharajas; the might of the British Raj; and an industrious people driving a flourishing trade route through to the ports of Gujarat, mingled with soothsayers and dedicated devotees alike. Sights and sounds all around seem to bring history to life. About a kilometre and a half southwest of the Bikaner Junction railway station, lies the old city surrounded by a seven-kilometre-long eighteenth-century wall accentuated by five gates—the main entrance being the triple-arched Kothe Gate.

A beautiful red-stone arched gate with trellis windows on walls that run out from it in both directions, imbued with handmade carvings still peeking from the domed roof of the archway, Kothe Gate is a sight to behold. On one side of the gate are intricately constructed Rajput havelis, while through the archway you can see the bustling Bhujia Bazaar on the other side. Kothe Gate delicately forms a beautiful barricade separating the old city from the new.

Strolling through the narrow, winding lanes of the bazaar gives a picturesque view of the streets lined with little hole-in-the-wall shops selling samosas and kachoris (varieties of fried dumplings filled with potatoes and spices), always served with heaps of freshly fried bhujia. The atmosphere is filled with the delicious aromas of bhujia, snacks and sweets, building a deep anticipatory tug of hunger.

No forms of transport, aside from cycles and an occasional errant motorbike, are anywhere to be seen inside the bazaar. Once inside, you are transported to an older time, when traders travelled by foot, horseback and bullock carts, bringing their goods to a market such as this one to make their fortunes. Unlike the busy streets of Chandni Chowk, the crowds of Bikaner have a certain laidback air about them, as though people have all the time in the world to stroll through these streets and savour the sights and smells of the place before making their purchases.

In every nook and corner of the bazaar, *halwais* or professional sweet makers, are producing piles of fried, delectable and addictive bhujia. Their hands move swiftly as they skim boiling oil that is bubbling over the tops of deep-frying karahis or pans, pulling freshly fried bhujia through a specially designed, perforated disc-like ladle. The action needs practised skill as a skim too deep might result in burnt painful hands and a skim too far from the top will leave the bhujia un-tossed. Yet, they work with a languishing nonchalance that only comes from years of practice. 'In the beginning, working with hot oil to remove the bhujia felt like torture, but with time one gets used to it,' said Chhote Ram, the owner of a small sweets and snacks shop, while proudly showing off hardened scabs on his hands.

'Bhujia sells,' he says, as if justifying the pains of making the snack. 'It is good business. Here, even a one-year-old child eats bhujia with every meal. It's a staple.' The demand for bhujia is evident in the fact that there are over 300 small bhujia shops and local brands in Bikaner alone. Locals treat it like a prerequisite to every meal, as if the people have been eating this form of bhujia for centuries.

Around 1885, during the reign of the benevolent Maharaja Dungar Singh, the first batch of bhujia was made in Bikaner. It was, in fact, well over a hundred years ago when bhujia made its foray into this market! It is in these very streets of Bhujia Bazaar that the first Haldiram shop was set up and has now been collecting dust for decades. Yet, the story doesn't quite start here. Across the street, opposite that very shop stands an older shop by the name of Bhikharam Chandmal. It is on the floor of this tiny, dingy workshop that the 'magic' we now know by the name of 'Haldiram's bhujia' began to take form.

## The Seeds of an Empire

Haldiram's grandsons, current owners of the family business entities in Bikaner, Nagpur, Kolkata and Delhi, inherited many of their grandfather's admirable genetic traits, but they certainly received the short end of the stick when it came to physique! These men, all shorter than 5' 5", have been endowed with Haldiram's business legacy and vigour, but lost out on his towering six-foot frame.

Haldiram was a tall, agile and fit man even in his seventies. At the ripe old age of seventy-two, he was seen riding his bicycle into town, checking on his storefronts and going about his daily chores. Family members remember him for his 'energy', his 'spirit' and his 'drive', and call him a 'man of action right until the day he died!' He didn't seem to ever slow down, and inspired awe in most around him. Not only was he tall in stature, but also tall when it came to his principles. 'Haldiram was old-school,' says his nephew, Poonam Chand. 'He had strong beliefs and he stood by his values and principles. He never strayed from his path. It is hard to find people like that these days.'

Independent, shrewd and with immense faith in himself and his ability to succeed, Haldiram—both during his lifetime and after—inspired generations of men and women in his family to excel and succeed in business. He not only left them a legacy in the form of the business they all so deeply cherish, but he also left a strong set of beliefs and principles for them to always fall back on.

Described as a man with a 'sober disposition' and 'serious mannerisms', apparently, Haldiram was never foolhardy and never wasted time on a joke! He was sincere about his work and dedicated to providing the best life he could for his family. Not known for his sense of humour, Haldiram inspired a combination of fear and awe in his sons and grandsons. Perhaps his seriousness was a result of the hard life he had led, or perhaps it came from having to grow up too quickly as boy—we may never find out. Nonetheless, it is clear that his dedication and devotion to the business laid down the foundation, the building blocks, for this snacks and sweets empire. However, the story didn't quite start with him.

It is a testament to how dearly the family keeps its heritage guarded and the value its members place on privacy that, to date, the media has not been able to accurately trace the beginnings of bhujia and this business. Most articles claim that Tansukhdas, Haldiram's great-grandfather, 'originally started the bhujia business'. However, family members claim that Tansukhdas never had anything to do with this business. He was, in reality, a small-time merchant in Bikaner, and the family itself doesn't have any record or memory of what his business might have been. Shiv Kishan Agarwal, Haldiram's oldest grandson alive and owner of the Nagpur unit admits, 'Tansukhdas never made bhujia. I don't think bhujia was popular in his time, or had even made a foray into the public sphere. He was a small-time businessman and whatever he sold, it was definitely not bhujia!' The story of bhujia definitely predates Haldiram, though, its alleged original founder never enjoyed even a tenth of Haldiram's fame, fortune and appreciation within the family.

Ganga Bhishen Agarwal, aka Haldiram, was born at a glorious time in Bikaner, when progress was the new theme song in town and Bikaner was beginning to evolve from the rural desert sprawl that it was into a flourishing trade town. He was the grandson of one Bhikharam Agarwal, son of Tansukhdas Agarwal, a poor and unimaginative merchant living in the Bachaut Ka Mohalla area in Bikaner.

Married young, Haldiram's grandfather was straddled with the responsibility of a wife and two sons, when his grandson Ganga Bhishen announced his arrival into the world with the usual loud perfunctory wail of newborns. In those days, boys became men as early as ten years of age. Before they knew it, they were married, and dutifully, they began adding to the population soon after. Bhikharam was himself a young man of just thirty-three when his grandson made a grand entry into the world in 1908! While this might come as a surprise to the millennials and youth of today, it was the norm in those times. In fact, many rural Marwari families even today marry off their sons and daughters very early. While *balika vadhu* (child marriage) is shocking to the modern Indian, it is still the harsh reality of young girls with Marwari roots living in rural areas.

The birth of his grandson was definitely a burden for Bhikharam. With the weight of the world on his shoulders, Bhikharam was desperate to find a new means of making enough money to feed the multiple mouths in his house. He seems to have had a small shop selling goods that nobody in the family today remembers, barely earning enough for family members to sleep content, with their bellies full. It was in this meagre manor that our legend was born.

In spite of the tough beginnings, Haldiram was a bright, cheerful kid with an enterprising spirit. Always helpful around the house, he seemed to take the initiative with most chores and tasks. He and his younger brothers, Mohanlal Agarwal and Kishan Gopal Agarwal, spent many a hot, dusty afternoon playing in the street in front of their house. His mother had stopped addressing him by his real name since he was little, and the nickname that she had dotingly given him—Haldiram—stuck on forever. While he was a favourite among all relatives because of his responsible demeanour, he was closest to his aunt, Bikhi Bai. The kids fondly called her Bikhi Bua.

Bikhi Bua only visited Bikaner during festivals and spent a few days at a time with her *maika* (parental home) at the house in Bachaut Ka Mohalla. Having been married into another Marwari merchant family, it was her duty to live with her in-laws and serve them. It so happened that Bikhi Bua's mother-in-law made a rugged, fat and firm form of bhujia as a snack at home, which Bikhi Bua prepare for Haldiram and his brothers during her visits. Everybody at home loved that spicy, tasty snack! Shiv Ratan Agarwal, Moolchand's second son and Shiv Kishan's younger brother, also the owner of the Bikaner unit, says about the time, 'There were hardly a handful of families that made that bhujia [fat and soft] at the time and even fewer that sold it.'

Bua, in introducing the family to the snack, had unwittingly set wheels in motion that forever changed the fates of this family and the history of Bikaner itself. An invisible player, she never received the credit she deserved for sowing the first seeds of bhujia in the Haldiram family, but her loyalty helped the family through one of its toughest phases, giving them the initial tools that later made them the magnates that they are today.

The immediate success of Bikhi Bua's bhujia with this young audience forced Bhikharam and his wife to learn how to make it just to keep the kids happy when Bua was away! Somewhere between 1908 and 1918, Bhikharam, realizing its potential, began making larger quantities of 'fat bhujia' to sell at his shop in Bhujia Bazaar. The initial sales were for a few measly paise per kilo. The bhujia was spooned into small paper funnels made from old newspapers. The product didn't exactly make waves but it brought him a little extra cash to keep his family just about fed and warm in the winters. The man who first started making and selling bhujia within the Agarwal family, Bhikharam Agarwal is the son of that Tansukhdas, who has always received unwarranted credit from the press for starting the bhujia business.

As a child, Haldiram was always found hovering near the *chula*, asking if the ladies needed any help with the fire pit. The little house was too small to accommodate an actual kitchen space, because of which the women had resourcefully carved out a corner for cooking in the living room. According to relatives, Haldiram would take on odd jobs such as chopping, cleaning and kneading, and gradually began to display an increasing interest in the bhujia-making process. In 1919, when Haldiram was just an innocent eleven-year-old, his father and grandfather decided that he was man enough to take on responsibilities of his own and got him married to Champa Devi. His wife, a young bride no older than nine, was not much of a companion at the time. Unable to truly grasp what they had gotten themselves into, the 'child couple', Haldiram and Champa, began their journey, which would last fifty years, together as husband and wife. In an earnest attempt to take his new responsibilities seriously, Haldiram began looking for ways in which he too could contribute to the family income.

When Bikhi Bua visited next, Haldiram was a young man, ready to make his mark in the world. At age twelve, he sat with her, intent on mastering the art of making bhujia and be the best at it. Making bhujia in those days was a task seeped in backbreaking, dangerous work. They used wooden ladles to pour in the batter into large woks, skimmed the oil with their bare hands on to thick, perforated, underdeveloped discs, scooped the bhujia up and placed it on old newspapers to dry. Haldiram overcame his fear of getting burnt, and learnt to deal with the hot oil; a feat that he accomplished in a mere fifteen-to-twenty-day period. Practice makes perfect, and boy did he practise! Legend has it that he made several batches a day, and within those initial few days, he had almost as many scabs on his hands as veteran halwais and snack makers today.

With Haldiram adding to the production, the family began making a little more money. The boy soon became a part of his grandfather's business and went to the shop daily. He was hard-working and ambitious; taking on greater responsibilities rapidly. However, what differentiated Haldiram from his grandfather was that he wasn't easily content with making a few paise per sale of bhujia, nor was he impressed by the taste and quality of their product. He wanted more, and this driven boy demonstrated unmatched resourcefulness and an uncanny appreciation of the customer's tastes for those times and meagre means.

'When Haldiram had an idea, he followed it through to the end,' said his nephew, Poonam Chand, now approximately sixty-five years old. The two simple yet significant changes that he made to bhujia revolutionized the product and turned it into the delectable, irresistible snack that it is today. The bhujia that Bikhi Bua had taught him to make was made with dough that was a mixture of *besan*, or chickpea flour, and *moth ki dal*, a lentil grown in Rajasthan. Moth ki dal was a staple with the Rajasthanis. They ate lentil curry filled with moth; or dry vegetable dishes mixed in it; or fried snack balls rolled in it. Almost every meal had something made from moth. This has to do with Rajasthan's geography, especially of the region of Marwar that was not endowed with fertile soil. The moth plant, surprisingly, does well in the desert and is available in abundance, making itself by necessity a local favourite. Yet, Bikhi Bua's bhujia had mostly besan in the dough, as besan gave it better consistency and was easier to fry. Contrary to his mentor's teachings, Haldiram refused to take the easier way out. He figured that if the bhujia were made from moth, people would simply find it irresistible. They would then buy the product not only because it filled their stomachs, but also because they couldn't get enough of the taste. In his youthful imagination, this immediately translated into higher sales and thereby a lot more money for the family. With a lot of determination and refusing to take no for an answer, the young *padawan* made a version of bhujia with moth and sold it separate from the family's original 'moti' bhujia at the same shop. Rapidly, its popularity grew and within a week, he was racing to match his production with the overwhelming demand.

Immensely impressed and convinced of the young man's insight into the hearts and penchants of the customers,

Bhikharam did not challenge Haldiram's next ingenious idea. Blessed with an intuitive understanding of spices and their flavours, Haldiram set out to explore the true definition of 'delicious' when it came to bhujia for his customers. He figured that if the bhujia could be crispy and crunchy, it would add to the fun element of eating it and satisfy the customer's need for a quick bite. To make the bhujia thin and crunchy, he needed to dilute the batter further. He also needed a perforated mesh with holes tiny enough for the outcome to be light, skinny and crispy, closer to the bhujia we know today. In spite of his busy schedule at the shop, Haldiram found the time to endlessly wander the market to identify the right mesh maker. When found, it is said that he spent hours with the mesh maker, overseeing the hammering and puncturing of the thin sheets of steel, to ensure the holes would be small enough and the mesh curved just right to serve the purpose.

Energized by innovative ideas that constantly sprang to his mind, it is said that the young Haldiram began many 'bhujia experiments' in his spare time. A keen sense of smell and taste helped guide this young magician to blend just the right spices in the right amounts while seasoning the bhujia. A year and multiple batches later, his thin, crispy, moth bhujia was ready to be taken to the market.

The new bhujia was an instant winner. Haldiram got his first sweet taste of success as the sales grew to more than anything the family had ever seen! Customers would come to the shop and ask especially for 'Haldiram's bhujia', and buy not only more often, but in greater quantities too! It was the beginning of young Haldiram's fame, and little did he know how much of it he was going to get!

'One more *muthi* of Haldiram's bhujia! One more handful, please!' The crowd gathered in throngs!

'It sold for 5 paise per kilo, which in those days was a lot of money for this commodity, especially since 64 paise made a rupee at the time,' said Shiv Kishan, Haldiram's oldest living grandson at seventy-five years of age. Soon, the demand for his product grew and everybody from rich seths (upper-class businessmen) to humble peasants drooled at the prospect of tasting 'Haldiram's bhujia'.

The shop was busy morning, noon and night, and the Agarwal men sweated their days away making and selling bhujia. As his bhujia began to gain popularity locally, merchants all the way from Kolkata, Assam and across Rajasthan too started to stop by to purchase 'Haldiram's bhujia' on their way home from business in Bikaner. When asked why this particular bhujia was so popular, every living family member has unanimously delivered one response sans hesitation—'*swad se bharpoor*', while smacking their lips. I don't think there is a term in the English language that exactly encapsulates their sentiment; yet, 'chock-full of delicious flavour' might just come close to describing it.

A scrawny lad of twelve, Haldiram was already well known in Bhujia Bazaar. Though his innovative bhujia was sold at his grandfather Bhikharam's shop, it was evident that it was Haldiram's product that the customers truly loved. At an age and era when education was scarce and poverty was abundant in rural India, and core business concepts and management fundas were just about being developed by some of the brightest business minds in the Western world, little Haldiram instinctively understood the value of customer centricity.

Unlike other paltry businessmen of his time, he didn't lose his head by the sudden surge in cash flow. In spite of the scarcity that he lived in, and the daily grind, this adolescent actually stopped to think and question the very basis of their business. He wanted to truly understand what would make the customers happy, identify ways in which product quality could be improved and thereby ultimately focus on attaining customer loyalty by delivering on their needs rather than resting his laurels on immediate sales. In retrospect, this could be seen as evidence of his strategic foresight. He did this by continuously experimenting with flavours and textures, and studying how customers reacted to different samples. However, at a deeper level, what Haldiram was portraying was an intense pride in what he did. This is the cornerstone of his empire, his legacy. It is rumoured that Haldiram preached quality right from this 'green around the ears' age of twelve, until when he died aged seventy-two in 1980.

Haldiram's initial success might have contributed to his lifelong commitment to quality and customer satisfaction. He strongly believed that success could be achieved only by providing customers with the best products, thereby ensuring their loyalty. He understood early on, the need to sell the best product to the customer regardless of what anybody else in the market was doing. Innovation for him was about making customers happy and achieving his highest potential, as opposed to just a competitive reaction to other products in the market. The enthusiastic and inexperienced move to produce a slightly different commodity helped him and his grandfather to not only attach slightly higher prices to the product, but also to create a barrier that other shopkeepers found hard to break down. They achieved all this at that early stage where the scale of production had not given them an edge in the market yet. Even today, a century later, when Bikaner alone has over 300 locally branded bhujia shops, and the product has been awarded the status of 'Bikaneri bhujia', Haldiram is a clear market leader with over 20 per cent market share in snacks, leaving the rest of the bhujiawalas to play catch-up.

In the streets of Bikaner, one could see bhujia heaped up in tiny shops in big *boris*, or jute bags, and sold in newspapers rolled into serving cones. This sumptuous fried snack was a generic food with no special packaging or marking; it was referred to as bhujia by everyone in Bikaner who sold it, bought it or ate it. Haldiram, due to his innovative approach and undeniable superior taste, had begun to receive some special recognition from customers. Yet, ambitious and dissatisfied with the status quo, the youngster had more elaborate plans for his bhujia.

Haldiram's innovation was not just limited to the making of his beloved bhujia. The young legend seemed to be somewhat of a marketing genius as well, demonstrating an uncanny understanding of the importance of brand associations, salience and resonance with customers. He perhaps wanted his bhujia to mean more than any other commodity in the snacks market. To that effect, he wanted customers to feel like they were doing something more than just munching on a snack when they bought his bhujia. Maybe he hoped they would feel prominent, worthy and possibly even royal. And so, he named the bhujia 'Dungar sev' after the well-loved maharaja of Bikaner, Dungar Singh.

Dungar Singh (1872–87), a courageous and forward-looking maharaja for those times, was known for his desire for a modern administration. He was the first Indian king to introduce a police force, establish the state's first hospital, and it was he who ensured that Bikaner was the first Indian princely state to introduce electricity in 1886. With his move to brand the bhujia, Haldiram differentiated 'Dungar sev' from its pale competitors by giving the bhujia a distinct name that encouraged and aided customers in easily recalling the product. He then took this naming exercise a step further by giving the bhujia a label that resonated with people and evoked feelings that were greater than those of merely 'snacking'! By associating the bhujia with a maharaja, his bhujia could immediately evoke feelings of self-respect and pride, thereby building greater brand resonance. Unknowingly, Haldiram initiated the Indian snack food industry into the world of branding to help the customer connect with his subconscious desire when deciding to purchase a product. In one single brilliant stroke, Haldiram both differentiated the product and gave it a recall value, while the royal association also gave the bhujia aspirational value.

What is amazing is that this teenager achieved all of his initial success with little to no formal education. In those days, people of Marwar hardly sent their children to school. Language was not a priority to this business-class community; however, an understanding of numbers and accounting was of utmost importance. Young children of five or six years of age were initiated into Marwari *padhai* by a local tutor. This Marwari tutelage consisted of a thorough education in counting, multiplication, logic, and profit and loss concepts. Children finished this schooling within a couple of years. What was highly interesting is that while regular school children are taught tables such as 2 x 2 = 4, Marwari children learn tables in decimal points, which they know by heart! This traditional society reveals a keen emphasis on mental maths. Any Marwari child could calculate 2.5 x 3.6 = 9 in a matter of seconds without putting pencil to paper. Ankita, Shiv Kishan's personal secretary and close family friend, confirms, 'They were taught so many mathematical tricks that they didn't have to think twice before calculating a complex problem and getting it right!'

Soon after 'school', Marwari children quickly learnt the connection between money and numbers, as this conservative society once again taught them a vital life lesson: the value of money. They would be given a paisa or two for doing odd jobs or helping with the business, thereby learning the concept of earning through skill, labour or service, and contributing to both the household and society. It is no wonder that most of India's famous businessmen are Marwaris. Haldiram began his journey with these very values ingrained in him. While these lessons enable Marwaris to gain an edge over other communities when it comes to business, Haldiram was especially endowed with a curious mind, a creative spirit and, above all, an optimistic courage that set him apart from other Marwari businessmen.

One often wonders about innovators and inventors, even those who create the littlest of originalities. How did they do it? When I was a teenager, I remember asking my father, 'I wonder how men discovered popcorn. Did they happen to throw a kernel into the fire and were surprised when it popped, or did early man simply happen to chance upon a kernel on a hot, dry day when it suddenly popped on the ground in front of him?'

Unlike the popcorn kernel, Haldiram's bhujia was no accident. His innovations helped create a staple food group for the people of Rajasthan and made waves right into the twenty-first century where bhujia is such a huge part of the Indian lifestyle that people sometimes substitute it for sabzi.

However, an empire was not erected on one innovation.

## The First Estrangement

Family and business have always been two sides of a coin for the Agarwals. In the beginning, business was a means of earning money to feed the many mouths of the family. Brothers, sisters, aunts and uncles all banded together to nurture the children. They lived under the same roof, they worked in the same shop, and broke bread together. There was no sense of I, me or mine—it was all us, we and ours.

During those initial years in the 1930s and '40s, the shop and the home were an extension of each other, part of their daily lives, their daily struggles and their daily triumphs. There was no question of ever abandoning the business. The business was a huge part of who they were—*businessmen* from a business family. The word business seems to be an adjective as important as Marwari to describe this tribe as a family, as a people and as a community.

Each family member, as they worked in the shop, added to the income of the family. What other members contributed in terms of odd jobs around the house and domestic chores helped in reducing costs for the family. This simple concept of productivity is the core philosophy behind their joint family system, and from this came their intense desire to cooperate with one another, be kind and helpful and take the initiative to contribute to the success of the family as a whole.

The entire family lived in a small house with four to five rooms in Bachaut Ka Mohalla. 'We must have been thirteen to fourteen people at least. We moved out of that house when I was three years old, in 1944,' said Shiv Kishan, a faraway look in his eyes. 'In those days, we didn't seem to need individual rooms, or even a specific, designated place to sleep. Everyone worked so hard that after a long day, we would simply plonk ourselves down wherever we found a spot and sleep our exhaustion away. In the mornings, we would be up at the crack of dawn, get ready and continue on our way.' Such were the simple trials of the family in the early decades of the Haldiram business. The rooms in the house were small and there was simply not enough space to house so many people. Family members would roll out *gaddas* and lay themselves down on the firm cotton bedding on a first come, first served basis. Some of them even slept out in the courtyard. Though one would guess that in the heat of the desert summers, sleeping outside under the shade of trees would have definitely been an attractive proposition. Without enough physical space, it was inescapable that family members got to know each other rather well. 'Work was always more important than having personal space. It was our joint mission to work together so we could eat together as a family,' Shiv Kishan added with a nonchalant shrug. Strength in unity was the core philosophy, which the Agarwals swore by.

If you think this paints too happy a picture, you are right to be cynical. Cracks soon began to show under this united facade. Trouble was brewing beneath the surface, and what were initially minor issues soon grew to become a chronic problem for Haldiram and his wife, Champa Devi. By 1944, at age thirty-six, Haldiram and Champa Devi had three sons, daughters-in-law and a three-year-old grandson. As mentioned, Haldiram's brothers, Mohan Lal and Kishan Gopal, were also married and living with their wives and children in the same house.

Somewhere along the way, a misunderstanding began to develop between the three sisters-in-law, and bad communication turned into a plague that no amount of maturity seemed to be able to cure. It was inevitable. Fourteen individuals, each endeavouring to squash their own individuality for the greater good of the household, were failing miserably, as humans often do under such pressure. The animosity within the cracks grew like a fungus in a deep fissure that the family could not get rid of.

The matter finally reached a tipping point when Champa Devi refused to live in the same house as her husband's brothers and their wives. Allegedly, Haldiram desperately reasoned with his wife, failing which, he asked for support from his elders and even tried to cajole his brothers into making peace. However, Champa Devi had made up her mind and obstinately took to fasting for seven days in order to be taken seriously. Haldiram was hesitant to leave his family; however, to preserve his wife's sanity, he finally decided to leave the family and walked out of the house and the business.

The details of how he survived following the falling-out saddled with three sons and a toddler for a grandson on the streets are a little hazy. Up until that point, Haldiram had been a devoted son and loyal contributor to the family income. However, now that he had separated from the family, he wasn't welcome to the business either! He had no means of livelihood from the moment that he had decided to estrange himself from his father and brothers. He had not put away any money or savings for himself,' said Shiv Kishan. 'Everything that was earned was earned for the whole family and went into the common pot of money. So when he separated, he was penniless.' There might have been a lot of bad blood—not only did Haldiram leave the house, but he left without a penny to his name or any monetary compensation for the multiple contributions he had made to the family business thus far.

One can't even begin to envisage his plight—out on the streets with his family, burdened with the responsibility of feeding multiple mouths, with no shelter, food or security. It would have been a gloomy predicament for most individuals to be reduced to utter destitution by a single decision. Did he feel regret or desperation at that point? We can only wonder. Nevertheless, Shiv Kishan claims, there was simplicity to those times and that his grandfather was a simple man with very few needs. According to him, Haldiram had a naive faith in the universe and truly believed that everything happened for a reason. When Haldiram would recount this story to his children and grandchildren many years later, Shiv Kishan confirms that he always said, 'I wasn't terribly worried. I always thought, whatever God sends my way is bound to be good for me.' This idealism and guilelessness is what kept him strong and positive during the tough times in his life. It is this attitude that possibly enticed lucky stars to favourably shine down on him during the most difficult phase of his life. As the old saying goes, good things come to those who wait.

Implausibly, as most real-life accounts often do, this tale takes a miraculous turn for the better. It was the middle of the day. There was a hot loo blowing, and in the harsh rays of the afternoon sun, Haldiram—disinherited, dreary and disheartened was aimlessly wandering the streets of Bikaner, wondering what work he could find to sustain his large family. Lost in his thoughts he almost missed the enthusiastic, emphatic calls of a familiar voice. 'Haldiram! Haldiram! HALDIRAAAAM!' someone shouted. He turned halfway just to make sure his ears weren't deceiving him, when he saw an average-looking man at a distance, frantically waving at him and urgently making his way towards him. Squinting his eyes, he recognized his old friend from the mohalla and felt the first burst of joy he had felt all week. 'Allah! Are you back?' he exclaimed, reaching out and giving his friend a hearty hug! He wasn't addressing God but simply speaking to his dear friend Allah Beli.

Allah Beli and Haldiram had been childhood friends and were close even though they had not met in years. While Allah had chosen to leave Bikaner's borders to seek his fortune, his friend had chosen to remain with his family. After much catching up, Haldiram finally informed Allah of his falling-out with the family and his current predicament. Ages ago, Haldiram had given Allah a loan of ₹200, a favour Allah had luckily not forgotten. On this once dreary day, Allah gratefully returned half of that money to his generous friend. We can only guess at why he didn't return the full amount—he might have taken advantage of his friend's desperation and tricked him into accepting only half the original amount or he might only have had that much money to his name. Whatever his motivations, this chance encounter that day had turned Haldiram's fortune around. With ₹100, Haldiram had the seed money to get himself and his family started. In spite of the recent falling-out, Haldiram had always been a family man and so attempting a peaceful do-over, he rented the small house next to his family's place and began brainstorming business ideas with his wife. Even though ₹100 was a lot of money in those days, it wasn't enough to start a shop of his own. As the family brainstormed over suitable sources of livelihood, an idea presented itself.

If there was one thing that Champa Devi did spectacularly well, it was cooking moong dal. Hers was a family favourite and mouth-wateringly delicious. Not one to underestimate the joys of a simple homemade meal, Haldiram applied his usual understanding of customer tastes and took to the streets armed with his wife's special concoction. Local workers in the area were always on the lookout for a cheap, delicious meal during their workday, and Champa Devi's moong dal was an instant hit with them. Healthy, hearty and hot, it served as the perfect meal for the working class. Haldiram had again fittingly identified the audience and made the perfect sales pitch by delivering the right product to the right customer. The man was born a marketeer. He instinctively understood the customer, a rare ability that most modern marketers spend years trying to acquire in school and on the job. He also leveraged his previous reputation of being an ace bhujia maker to win immediate trust from the customer who was more than willing to try a new product from this familiar snack seller. Within the week, sales were booming and Champa Devi and her daughters-in-law were hard at work, round the clock, trying to churn out enough of the moong dal. Within no time, Haldiram had become as successful as any street hawker selling off a cart could get, and there was once again food on the table for the family.

However, as any man born with an inimitable talent, the moong dal could only keep Haldiram satisfied for so long. He itched to go back to making and selling what he really loved—bhujia. Haldiram worked tirelessly, from dawn to dusk, walking the streets of Bhujia Bazaar to sell the moong dal and save enough money so that he could start a venture of his own. It never occurred to him to simply work for someone else. It was either the streets or running a business—that is all he had ever known. Moong dal was simply a source of livelihood. Bhujia was his first love. That is where his passion lay—and his destiny.

When he had just about enough money in his kitty, Haldiram went about setting the wheels in motion to do what he was born to do. He sought out Berundarji Kothari. Berundarji was a very powerful and wealthy landlord in Bikaner who also had a rich and flourishing clothing business in Kolkata. Haldiram had built a relationship based on mutual respect while working at the old shop with his father and grandfather. Berundarji had been a huge fan of Haldiram's bhujia and it was this fondness that Haldiram was counting on.

As a wealthy and renowned landlord in Bikaner, Berundarji also happened to be a trustee of a temple complex named Chintamani Mandir in Bikaner, which exists to this day. Haldiram, during his daily explorations of the city selling moong dal, had come to notice that a small shop within this complex had become vacant. He tried to talk to the local caretaker about renting it out but was met with considerable resistance. Through small talk with the workers in the area, Haldiram heard that the trustee of the complex was Berundarji. A meeting then became necessary. He struck a deal with Berundarji to be granted the right to rent the shop so he could set up a bhujia stall of his own.

It is said that Haldiram had never once in his life asked anybody for a favour or a loan. In order for that to be true, he must have done Berundarji a favour in the past or had some sort of arrangement with Berundarji in terms of profit-sharing from this shop to win the deal. Either way, the enterprising young man was soon the owner of a small shop in the Chintamani complex.

In the beginning, all he could afford was a tiny chula in the shop. Chulas, in those days, were highly rudimentary cooking stoves—an assemblage of bricks surrounding a narrow mud pit. Cooks often burnt wood as fuel in this pit. The room got hot and smoky, and the only outlet for the smoke was the front door. Chefs worked around the chula in spite of the heat and smoke. Very rarely did these tiny rooms have chimneys. Once this particular chula started burning in the small shop at the Chintamani complex, there was no looking back.

Every morning, Haldiram and his wife were up long before sunrise, at 2 a.m., like clockwork. Within the hour, both husband and wife would be at the shop; Champa Devi mixed the batter and kneaded the dough, while our master bhujia maker blended in the spices and prepared the actual bhujia himself. As the morning working hour beckoned, Haldiram would open shop, ready to serve his customers freshly made, warm bhujia direct from the chula. Whatever initial trepidation they might have felt at starting this new business and competing with their own family disappeared in the first few days. Word spread fast within Bhujia Bazaar that Haldiram was back—and so was his bhujia. His old customers flooded the shop in droves to buy the fresh bhujia and Haldiram was immensely relieved to witness how sorely his Dungar sev had been missed. While the original shop run by his grandfather, Bhikharam Chandmal, had also been selling bhujia, nobody in that house had been able to master Haldiram's delicious recipe! As word continued to spread, people began waiting in queues for the bhujia even while it was being made to make sure they got their share before Haldiram shut shop for the day. 'His customers were very particular about taste and were *shaukeen*,' said Shiv Kishan with a smile.

In the same year that he had broken away from his family and hit the streets penniless, Haldiram had wondrously rented a house, set up a new shop and regained his old fame.

For the next many years, maintaining and growing that shop was Haldiram's main ambition. He built his popularity around customer centricity and the quality of the product, compelling his sons and grandsons to adopt his principles for posterity. Being a man of strong beliefs, he led his life unwaveringly, based on values he held true for himself. According to his grandsons, not only did he lead by example but he was also a very loud and demanding personality. That, along with the fact that he was probably the only Agarwal over six feet tall, made him a rather imposing figure!

While he could be considered the father of bhujia, he also had several quirks that both endeared him to his family and also made for many an amusing tale to be shared with family and friends. Early in his life, Haldiram achieved a sense of self-discipline that many of us today fail to on a daily basis. He had a set routine—and boy did he stick to it! By 5 a.m., he would be done with his morning ablutions, have read the Gita, have said his prayers and done his exercise, ready to get to the shop and open the shutters. Being a staunch Jain, he ate his main meal of the day at 10 a.m. 'If the plate was not set before him at 10 a.m., sharp, he would simply skip the meal and not eat until right before sunset,' said Mahesh Agarwal, another grandson, shaking his head in mock exasperation. Sometime in his forties,

Haldiram had reconciled to getting to the shop by 7 a.m., and he stuck to that time no matter which city he was in and which son's shop needed to be opened. 'In the winters, at 7 a.m., it was still dark, the air heavy and misty-white. The entire marketplace remained shut until at least 9 a.m., when the nippy dew settled. However, Dadaji would insist on getting to the shop and sitting there with only a lonely lamp to give him company, shivering in the cold, knowing fully well that he would not see a single customer for at least another couple of hours!' recalls Manoharlal Agarwal, the owner of Haldiram's in Delhi, with a chuckle.

While notorious for his doggedness, Haldiram believed he had to keep his promise to his customers. They had been assured the shop would open at 7 a.m., and he was forever horrified at the rare possibility that a customer could come by and not find anyone there. He took pride in his word and believed in the old-fashioned tradition of keeping it. That was how loyalty to the initial brand was built, and it couldn't have had a more dedicated spokesperson! 'He considered customers to be equal to God,' said Manoharlal. 'He would always say, "God doesn't give me my house and money to support my family; my customers do. Whatever we sell to the customers, they must always feel that they have got their money's worth. That's why they come back".'

Haldiram had earned tremendous respect from the local community because of his values and his scruples. Many a day, he went to work by cycle-rickshaw. According to Mahesh Agarwal, 'He was so honest that every day before departing for home, he would ask the cashier at his own shop to give him 50 paise for travel expenses. Being the owner, he owed the cashier no explanations; however, he expected the cashier to make an account of all expenses regardless of the amount and who they were made by.' In spite of being the boss, Haldiram never expected special considerations from anybody, least of all his employees.

His humble attitude would at times even frustrate his sons. 'Once when Haldiram was returning to Bikaner after many productive months in Kolkata, his second son, Rameshwarlal, affectionately gifted his father a double silk vest, so that Haldiram could return to his home town looking very much like the proud and successful businessman that he was,' regaled Poonam Chand, with mild amusement. 'However, Rameshwarlal's hopes and enthusiasm were dashed when his father quite sternly asked him to return the "superfluous luxury item". You can imagine Rameshwarlal's disappointment,' said Poonam Chand dramatically. 'He tried to argue with his father. "We have nothing to worry about any more," he reasoned. Yet, Haldiram's simple response had been to remind his son that "their sweat and blood must always count for more than frivolities"!'

While having a great regard for personal labour and hard work, Haldiram always took his 'value for money' principle to new heights. Poonam Chand relates an incident to illustrate this: 'On one occasion, when everyone was returning home in rickshaws after visiting a friend, and there were many of us from both homes—Bhikharamji's as well as Haldiramji's—we took a couple of rickshaws. I remember Haldiramji's rickshaw was behind ours. It was a miserable day, engulfed in dark clouds and heavy rains, and the narrow gully was overflowing with knee-deep water. The poor rickshaw guy was peddling standing up with all his might, trying to get us home before it was impossible to ride any further. Nearing our house, we asked the rickshaw driver to drive up the sidewalk so that we could avoid the water and get home in a decent state. The rickshaw driver said it would cost an additional 25 paise and we struck a deal. However, when Haldiramji's rickshaw driver said the same to him, he was outraged,' said Poonam Chand, unable to stop grinning through the narration. 'I remember him muttering some profanities like he often did. Finally, he shocked us all by pulling up his dhoti, yanking off his shoes, and finally jumping into the knee-deep muddy water. He swiftly waded over to his house . . . all this to save a meagre 25 paise,' Poonam Chand continued, shaking his head incredulously.

Haldiram was creative, focused and hard-working, but like most perfectionists, he was also famous for having a short temper, a trait that many of his grandsons have come to inherit. He had faced numerous pressures and hardships from a young age, burdening his personality with not only a heavy dose of obstinacy, but also a righteousness that was hard to argue with. Add to that a deep desire to produce the perfect product, and we have the perfect formula for a few volcanic eruptions. The man had revolutionized how bhujia was made, and unless someone could truly show him a better way to do it, they had bloody well do it just as he had taught them. 'He would get very angry if something went wrong, if an ingredient was missing or something fell short in the final quality of the product,' said Shiv Kishan. A little hesitant, he then added, 'When Dadaji was in a rage, he would shout, and people around him would meekly listen till the tirade ended.' Where Shiv Kishan was conservative in his account of his grandfather's temper, his brothers readily admitted that on several occasions, Haldiram had spanked them for mistakes and impunity.

While Haldiram was a strict disciplinarian, his wife, Champa Devi, handled the family with a soft touch. 'She was a quiet, hard-working lady,' says Shiv Kishan. 'As tradition mandated, she kept her *ghunghat* (covering only the head) on at all times and rarely looked her husband or in-laws in the eye.' While this might seem contrary to the earlier picture of a woman stubborn enough to fast for seven days just to get her way, Champa Devi's humility, perseverance and devotion to her husband have been the highlights of her legacy. When Haldiram, stingy and responsible, held on tightly to his purse strings, 'it was Champa Devi who generously gave four-anna and eight-anna coins to us kids,' recalls Poonam Chand fondly.

For those times, Champa Devi had taken a very bold step when finally cracking under the pressure of living in a difficult family situation and demanding that her husband separate from the family. From the very moment that Haldiram took the step and decided to follow his own destiny, Champa Devi had toiled into the night to help her husband stand on his two feet. 'She was very supportive and silently took on endless responsibilities at home and at the back end of the shop. She always acted instantly in times of need and led by example, silently doing whatever needed to be done,' said Shiv Kishan. It is possible that she felt responsible, and even a little guilty, for forcing Haldiram to leave his family, but she was definitely relentless in her effort to contribute towards lessening his burdens. In taking her stance, she might have inadvertently been the root cause of the success behind this brand—by forcing Haldiram to embrace his creativity and discover his business acumen, as he struggled to become independent and self-sufficient without the support of his father and brothers.

Family members only remember her silent sacrifices like a vague protective cloud that would hover over them when she was alive. The same was the plight of Bikhi Bua, the inadvertent pioneer of the family's venture into bhujia and snacks. It seems to be a lamp post of the Marwari culture for women to have little or no significance within the family business. They were meant to be nurturers, constantly available to provide care and nourishment to the men and children. The Agarwals' lives, memories and history revolved around the men and have continued to do so well into the twenty-first century.

In spite of being a strict disciplinarian, Haldiram, like Champa Devi, had a soft spot for children, especially his grandchildren. His exterior might have seemed tough, but his grandchildren fondly remember all the time they spent with him during their childhood. 'We would rush home in the evenings knowing what was in store,' said Manoharlal with a smile. 'One or two of us would massage his feet while he amused the whole platoon with grand stories.' Apparently, Haldiram's stories lasted days, sometimes even weeks. He had certainly bought into the school of *The Arabian Nights* to keep his grandkids entertained. 'He would tell us about Vikramaditya, Raja Harishchandra . . . stories of kings and their empires and lessons to be learnt,' said Mahesh Agarwal.

Somehow, the key lesson that the stories focused on was quality. He vowed to never compromise on it and 'always operate with integrity to find success'. At times, the man behaved like a broken record when it came to sharing his morsels of wisdom. He would preach about saints and religion and talk of healthy eating and living habits. 'He was almost like a loudspeaker! The whole house would hear him giving these wise lectures and

feel sorry for the poor chap who was forced to stay and listen!'
Mahesh Agarwal recalls with a grin.

While he absolutely loved making his bhujia, his own
principles forbade him from snacking in between meals. He
would taste the final product professionally but never with
the motive of snacking. 'He did have a weakness,' Manoharlal
confessed with a twinkle in his eye. 'He was a sucker for good
kachori. There was a local kachori stand nearby and Dadaji
would quietly treat himself to the local delicacy. According
to him, it was the best he had ever eaten!' Having tasted the
wonderful kachoris at Haldiram's restaurant at South Extension
in New Delhi, one can't help but feel their mouth water at the
thought of his recommended kachori. Even though he was
highly principled, Haldiram also harboured a liking for chewing
tobacco, which he did whenever he could.

A simple, yet driven man, Haldiram never dreamed of how
far he or his legacy could go. He lived a life of discipline, devoted
and loyal to his family and his customers. His bhujia brought
him some fame in his lifetime, but his grandsons took his name
and legacy farther, beyond even the borders of the nation.
Haldiram was born around the same time that Maharaja Sadul
Singh, the last remaining king of Bikaner, was born. It is said
that an old and renowned soothsayer at the time proclaimed
that 'the Raja would be famous in Bikaner and would be known
and loved by his people, but this little boy (Haldiram) would
someday become world-famous, and everyone would know
his name', said Poonam Chand, remembering the lore his own
father had told him.

Whether a coincidence or a fact, the pundit had predicted
the future quite accurately, given that the Haldiram products

are today exported to almost a hundred countries. The journey began with the namesake himself in a dusty little desert town, only to travel with great velocity to Kolkata, Nagpur and Delhi, before claiming its spot in the international markets.

# PART II

# GREENER PASTURES

# A Golden Era

Ambition drives just as much as contentment lulls. Having established a self-sustaining business by the 1940s, Haldiram had settled into the peaceful existence of daily routine. While life was still hard, filled with long working hours, the anxiety that comes with having to prove oneself had been assuaged, and a lazy confidence had taken root. Haldiram's clan at Bachaut Ka Mohalla had a solid base and could finally enjoy the fruits of their labour in the form of hot meals, a warm hearth of their own, cosy beds and a loving close-knit family.

Compared to other local shops, their business was flourishing. Bhujia, that was once sold for 2 paise per kilo, had slowly made its way up to 5 paise, 10 paise and later 25 paise. The family was beginning to make more profits, and the initial struggle that came with setting up a new enterprise was beginning to dissipate. To handle the excess demand and keep the shop open longer hours, the family developed a rotation system. The men of the family took on all responsibilities for making and selling bhujia while the women toiled to keep the household running. Haldiram's shift began at two in the morning, when he began production in earnest and ended, eight hours later, at ten, just in time for his first meal of the day. Moolchand Agarwal, his oldest son, would take the next shift followed by Satyanarayan and Rameshwarlal Agarwal, the middle and youngest son respectively. And so, it would continue day after day, regardless of what day of the week it was. The concept of weekends did not exist back then, especially for businesses, which dealt with perishables, and in those days, bhujia still had a short shelf life and was sold in newspaper cones for instant consumption. People bought fresh food on almost a daily basis and so Haldiram's shop remained open to meet the needs of its customers.

They were selling 100–200 kilos of bhujia per week—compared with the over 1000 kilos per day of a single product produced at Haldiram's today, it may seem measly—which was a grand scale to operate at in the 1940s and early 1950s in the small town of Bikaner. With increasing demand, Haldiram and his sons built a small shed with three wooden stoves so that the four of them could work together in the back of the house. Being able to make bhujia simultaneously more than tripled production to 300–400 kilos of bhujia per week, and thus they could successfully meet customer demand.

By this time, there was a sense of pride and achievement within the Haldiram household. They were known in the community for the superiority of their product. Haldiram himself was deeply respected as a man of principles, and Moolchand, Satyanarayan and Rameshwarlal benefitted from the reputation their father had already built in Bikaner. Having avoided the struggle of setting up a business, they were already 'entitled' second-generation businessmen with family money and a potential inheritance, however small it might have been. While they assisted Haldiram in building the business, the risk they assumed was little, compared to the pressures that governed their father's work. 'Each generation claims the younger is softer, and in our case that has been true! While our fathers worked hard with Haldiramji, they weren't the true bearers of the burden to "feed the family"; he was. Similarly, I feel my struggles have been greater than my sons can imagine, but each does what he needs to in his time,' said the wise Shiv Kishan Agarwal.

While the current owners of the various business units were hesitant to share a lot of details about their fathers, through my journey interviewing for this book, it was interesting to glean that Haldiram's three sons were showing distinct personalities even at that early a stage. In an indirect manner, these differences paved the path for the bitter separation and the court battles the family would fight in the years to come.

Early on, the youngest—Rameshwarlal—showed signs of greater drive than his elder brothers—Satyanarayan and Moolchand—evident in the way he later took ownership for the move to Kolkata and single-handedly managed business there till he passed away in 1991. Rameshwarlal had also inherited the same keen sense of taste and skill when it came to making bhujia that his father had exhibited years before. He was dedicated to doing his job well during his shift and enjoyed the art of bhujia-making as much as managing the sales and operational aspects of the business.

Moolchand, on the other hand, is often described as the 'peace-loving' brother who lacked true ambition and vision. A true people person, Moolchand loved socializing with his friends and spent hours chit-chatting with them. Laid-back and not overly ambitious, Moolchand preferred playing the counter salesman. He would sit at the shop, charm customers and sell bhujia as long as he didn't have to actually make it.

Knowing his heart, Haldiram and the family never really pressured Moolchand into doing what he wasn't born to do—unnecessary labour. However, during times when demand was unmanageable, he would be forced to hunker down and get his hands dirty with the dough and the hot oil. Most other times, his younger brother Satyanarayan, who worshipped him, would cover for him by taking over his bhujia-making shifts. Moolchand had a Tom Sawyer–like aversion to working but had a charming way about him that inspired cooperation. His effortless ability to understand human nature and inspire trust and understanding between various parties played a huge role in maintaining peace within the family for the years up until his death. While his sons are not above calling him out on his idle lethargy, he is credited for 'keeping the family together' during times of conflict. However, as most diplomatic men, he lacked the passion vital to lead his sons and command their respect.

In the 1940s and '50s, all the brothers managed that one shop together with their father, Haldiram. The profits were enough to sustain the entire family, and while Haldiram's dreams had gotten the family this far, the sons hadn't quite begun to dream big. They did not see themselves taking over their own state of Rajasthan, to say nothing of taking over Kolkata or the rest of India. The family was satisfied with being the most popular bhujia shop in Bhujia Bazaar in Bikaner and might have even coasted on that little business for the rest of their lives if opportunity had not come knocking at the right time. This is evident in Shiv Kishan's take on their father's ambition. When asked if Moolchand was perhaps driven by dreams outside of the family business since he wasn't motivated by making bhujia, Shiv Kishan vehemently disagreed, saying, 'My father never thought big. He simply coasted along in life and was happy in its simplicity. He never wanted more than he had. Family and friends mattered to him more than the sense of achievement that came from running a business.' Almost mirroring Shiv Kishan's opinion on Moolchand's lack of strategic foresight, Prabhu Shankar Agarwal, owner of the Kolkata business and eldest son of Rameshwarlal, said of his father, 'Babuji never really dreamed about the future. He always lived in the harsh reality of the present dealing with everyday fires. That was him—hard-working and committed, but never a visionary.'

The stirrings for the move to Kolkata began in the early 1950s, though nobody quite remembers the exact timelines. Sometime between 1950 and '55, Haldiram went to Kolkata for his dear friend Bhanwarlal Rampuria's son's wedding. It was a magnificent affair and Haldiram, overwhelmed with affection for his childhood mate, made bhujia for all the wedding guests over the course of the festivities. In the gregarious and plentiful atmosphere of the wedding, compliments flew generously as one by one the guests oohed and aahed, relishing the taste of the bhujia. Soon, people were placing bulk orders for the tasty bhujia to be sent from Bikaner. Once the daughter-in-law had been blessed and welcomed to her in-laws' place, as was the custom, and the excitement had simmered down, Bhanwarlal sat his old friend down and told him that he had been blessed with a wonderful skill. Bhanwarlal believed bhujia could make waves in Kolkata with its unique, spicy and crispy flavour, especially since no snack of the variety then existed in the eastern capital of the country.

In all the revelry surrounding the Kolkata wedding, Haldiram had learnt one thing—the Bengalis had good taste! Most wedding guests had loved his bhujia, which made Haldiram enormously happy and stoked his ambition somewhat—it was this secret flair of ambition which his friend Bhanwarlal probably exploited. Bhanwarlal assured Haldiram of the immense potential of expanding to Kolkata in terms of the market's readiness. Being a local businessman himself, he recognized the potential of the current customer demand and believed the time was right for the Haldiram brand to be a first-mover in the space. He was certain that they could monopolize the customer's 'share of plate' as well as their hearts! Being a true Marwari, Haldiram was also highly committed to his relationships with others, and relied on long-term contacts to run a thriving business. Knowing that his friend would connect him with suppliers, landlords and cheap labour probably also lessened Haldiram's fear of risk. Kolkata, by that point, had a growing community of Marwaris, and the thought of being able to set up shop ensconced by the warm security of a close-knit fraternity gave Haldiram heart. In the end, Haldiram's compass as a businessman recognized the opportunity at hand, and the decision to move was made. Resolute, he travelled back home to Bikaner with promise in his heart and purpose in his step.

Even though he was initially hesitant, after hours of conversation, Haldiram was finally convinced that they had to expand the bhujia business to Kolkata. As a veritable city of foodies, who better to serve the Bengalis than Haldiram, master at identifying customer preferences and ace at mixing spices? Once back in Bikaner, Haldiram broached the subject with the entire family. Family members followed a similar trajectory of hesitation, posing the very same questions Haldiram had faced in Kolkata. However, having been through this rigorous exercise himself, Haldiram was able to allay their fears and convince them to unanimously vote for the expansion to Kolkata.

In spite of the fact that the family business was initially built through the bold steps of young Haldiram, over the years, the family has also demonstrated a trend for hesitating in the face of taking risks that could aid the business in growing too quickly. At various points in their history, they have often taken smaller tentative steps when they could have taken long strides, acting with caution rather than in confidence. This is evident in their deep deliberation over the opportunity to move to Kolkata. This tendency to protect their heritage along with the various family conflicts have been the blunt side of the razor-sharp sword they wielded, dampening their successes at times and holding them back from becoming greater than what they are.

The ambition started with Haldiram but trickled down through the generations to the youngest, fourth generation of the family, currently responsible for this remarkable business in partnership with the third generation. These men, the current owners and heirs of the Kolkata, Nagpur and Delhi outfits, are driven by the need to protect their business from unnecessary risk at the cost of snail-like growth or even stagnancy. Haldiram's initial hesitation to move to Kolkata stemmed from a similar need to protect his livelihood and the source of the greatest part of his identity. He feared the unknown. This wasn't a mere fear of failure, but it was compounded by the dreaded sense of losing a foundation pillar through that failure. The risk too seemed huge. While Haldiram was famous in Bikaner, he would be virtually unknown in the big, bustling town of Kolkata. He also staunchly believed in not taking loans, so moving to Kolkata would mean investing hard-earned family savings in the venture. 'What if it doesn't work out? What if it is a colossal waste of resources, time and effort? What if in the process we lose everything?' This need to conserve their socio-emotional wealth led the Agarwals to make several sup-optimal decisions throughout their history. However, the move to Kolkata seemed destined.

## The Might of Marwars

The desert shimmers like an ocean of golden dust in the severe brightness of sunrays in Rajasthan. Everything glitters in that vast expanse. Light glints off the folds of cacti and sparkles in the tiny mirrors sewn on to the dresses of women and the overcoats of men. However, all that glitters is not gold—and the ancestors of Marwar would eagerly confirm that today if they could. The Marwar region includes the central and western parts of Rajasthan, the state's most infertile terrain. The word 'Marwar' itself is derived from the Sanskrit word '*Maruwat*', meaning 'desert'.

Today, Rajasthan is one of the most popular tourist destinations in India with travellers flocking in from around the world to admire its endless sand dunes and formidable forts, frolic with women in pretty Rajasthani mirror-work skirts, to ride camels and buy exotic hand-carved furniture for their homes, reminding them of their fantastical travels. However, till about fifty years ago, when the Indira Gandhi Canal was built to water the infertile land, the desert was barren and the people of Marwar cursed with earth that would not grow any crops for hundreds of years.

Most of north India's wealth came from the fertility of its lands; however, the people of Rajasthan had been denied this heavenly gift. India was a farming country and agriculture has been the backbone of its economy for hundreds of years. The Marwari people, though born in dust, had over the years learnt to refine whatever skills they possessed like iridescent diamonds polished from the rough. Instead of resigning themselves to a life of poverty and misfortune brought on by having been born on infertile land, they evolved into highly resourceful and skilled businessmen in order to survive the rigours of the desert. They were industrious and organized themselves into a community of proficient merchants who had instituted a tradition of leaving their family in their ancestral villages to venture out into faraway lands to make their fortunes.

Marwaris usually have a strong sense of family and community. It is not uncommon for a Marwari who has become a successful businessman to invite his unemployed relatives and neighbours from his village to join him as he expands the business opportunity. These ties last for generations after migration, and are a recurrent theme in the Haldiram family's journey too over the last hundred years. Through this self-perpetuating practice, Marwaris have built close-knit communities wherever they have migrated, preserving their traditional values while learning to adapt to new cultures. Historically, Marwaris travelled outside their ancestral homes seeking economic advancement, which forced them to be the outsiders in every new community. This propelled them to develop the ability to negotiate and compromise with the natives in these new territories.

Diplomatic as well as skilled in business, Marwaris began to enjoy greater status within the larger Indian community. While these businessmen prided themselves on their ability to adapt to different cultures, they have nurtured their traditional beliefs about women, family and business through the ages. Traditionally, women were not educated in Marwari families and almost never trained to work in the family business—a tradition devoutly followed by the Haldiram men even in the twenty-first century. Denied a constructive role in business, while women have rarely influenced the enterprise's growth, the men have held that the women have certainly had a hand in changing the course of the family business's history by promoting differences within the family and forcing the divisions. While this doesn't hold true in the case of the move to Kolkata, it definitely has its place in the later chapters of the family's history.

Marwaris' insistent devotion to their family and traditional practices have made them ignore modern education for several decades. While it may be a generalization, as a community, they have always put greater stock in practical knowledge, shrewdness and the mastery of mental maths rather than formal education. So it's not surprising to note that when Haldiram, his sons, Rameshwarlal and Satyanarayan, and seventeen-year-old grandson—Moolchand's eldest son, Shiv Kishan, went to Kolkata, none of them had been educated beyond the sixth grade, none could speak English or Bengali, and the only advantage they possessed was the knowledge of running a successful business that they had gained while setting up the bhujia shop in Bikaner. This has been the hallmark of the family where even the third generation of this family, who are the current owners of the Kolkata, Nagpur and Delhi outfits, have barely been educated beyond the eighth grade. And yet, they have all flourished, succeeded and built businesses that now bring in millions of dollars in revenues annually.

The year 1564 marks the earliest record of Marwaris in Bengal: during the reign of Suleman Kirani, Rajput soldiers under Akbar's flag camped there, as stated by the author Taknet in his book, *The Marwari Heritage*. The contract to supply essentials to the soldiers was conferred to the merchants of Marwar. Soon, these Marwari seths became a revered upper class in society, and rulers from different states in India began to compete with each other to entice the seths to set up businesses in their towns. Marwari seths were given armed protection for their convoys, and charters for the construction of schools, temples and wells. They were even offered immunity from customs, search and seizures, as well as criminal prosecution. Many privileges were bestowed upon them, their opinions given weight, their cooperation of utmost importance to states, as rulers were dependent on the merchant community for economic support. Historically, Marwari seths have generously given back to their communities in the form of charitable institutions. Many of the nation's most prestigious institutions—including Birla Institute of Technology, IITs, Ruia College and Poddar School—are a result of Marwari benevolence.

And so, in 1955, Haldiram's migration to Bengal was set in motion. The Agarwals went into this foray with the sound knowledge of history and an existing strong community of Marwari businessmen in Kolkata. The Agarwals held their family close and their friends closer; these associations brought the vehicle of opportunity to their doorstep, nourishing the family and supporting the business. While Moolchand, his wife and three younger sons stayed on in Bikaner, Shiv Kishan, his eldest son, and Rameshwarlal made the trek across the desert with Rameshwarlal's wife Kamala Devi in the hopes of helping the head of the family, Haldiram, set up a new arm of the business. The young Shiv Kishan, with a keen sense of taste and smell, and a natural at making bhujia, was proud to be chosen and eager to make his mark in the world of business. Satyanarayan too, along with his wife and children, dutifully accompanied his father to extend a helping hand where necessary.

Abhey Rawat Bachawat, a dear friend of Haldiram's from his childhood days, immediately helped the family set up home at No. 3, Harpudo Gali, Bhurjo Dalal Street in Kolkata. It was almost like déjà vu. Once again, the apartment was tiny, and the huge family uncomplainingly took to settling in and creating a workshop space to make bhujia. Within a week, production had begun, and bhujia was being made on wooden stoves in the rudimentary workshop. The men would pile up freshly made bhujia on to large dishes and march the streets of the Bhurjo Dalal area with their wok-laden cart, selling bhujia in newspaper cones to workers and local merchants. The old strategy worked well, and the delicious bhujia soon won the hearts and loyalties of the local community that had never before eaten such a delectable snack. In spite of having already set up a flourishing shop in Bikaner, the family had not been spoilt by their success and continued to remain in touch with their humble roots. Driven by ambition, and humbled by the daunting task ahead of them, they quickly took to starting once again at the bottom. They took their status of street vendors in the humidity of Kolkata's busy markets in stride.

Their network of Marwari friends spread the news, and bhujia soon gained popularity in Kolkata. Workers and traders alike began to recognize the various spots the cart visited at different times of the day, and rushed to their favourite snack.

The family was definitely making greater profits in Kolkata. Being a bigger city with higher standards of living, they were able to sell bhujia at ₹1.5 per kilo as opposed to 25 paise in Bikaner. The cost per kilo was Re 1, and so for each kilo sold, the family made a profit of 50 paise. Over the months, they saved enough to be able to rent a shop by the end of their first year in Kolkata. Abhey Rawat spotted an empty shop on Kalakar Street with a rent of ₹50 per month. The shop was extremely small—8 sq. ft, but it was a start. Haldiram could have only a couple of counter tops to showcase his product and a couple of people to help out in the shop. They had already been selling 150–200 kilos a day on the streets and hoped that their sales and production would increase at the shop front.

Throughout the 1950s, whenever Haldiram needed skilled craftsmen, he sent for a *karigar* from Bikaner—distant relatives and friends from his village back home—to help with the daily production of bhujia as well as work in the shop selling his product. In Kolkata, the family also started trading under the name 'Haldiram Bhujiawala'. The first decade was spent growing the business, building trust and credibility in the community and strengthening their network with fellow Marwaris and other businessmen. While they took pains to become a part of Kolkata's cultural backdrop, even today the Bengali locals consider them outsiders. Some locals in the city admit, 'The Haldiram folks are not Bengali. They are different. They are businessmen.' Kolkata, a city filled with artists, writers and revolutionaries, had been forced to squeeze in and make room for businessmen for centuries, subconsciously acknowledging that perhaps shrewdness and cunning was genetic, and reluctantly conceding that these outsiders were a necessary component for their economic sustenance.

* * *

Within the next decade, the shop grew to three times its original size. By 1967, it was 25 sq. ft in area and a thriving centre of business on Kalakar Street. While the size of the shop itself had only increased three times, the sales had increased by more than 100 per cent on an annual basis since 1956. Travellers, traders and locals alike had begun to recognize the Haldiram brand name, and many were definitely aware of the snack called bhujia. All this while, the family had no inkling of marketing tools such as advertising, billboards or posters, and were solely relying on the good old word of mouth. As their reputation grew, they began diversifying their product lines based on the varied palates of the Bengalis.

The first product that the Agarwals attempted to make outside of bhujia was the Bengali mixture. It all started with some local Marwari friends singing praises of this light and crispy mixture. Accepting the challenge, Shiv Kishan and his uncle, Rameshwarlal, hit the workshop, aka their personal laboratory, and began tasting the mixture to sniff out its secrets and reveal all the ingredients that went into making it. Multiple iterations and many days later, they hit upon a concoction that they were highly satisfied with. Pilot production of this tasty snack began, and the Agarwals began to offer a limited amount at their shop. Uninitiated into modern marketing practices, they uniquely began by allowing customers to take away little samples of the mixture to taste. Soon, the mixture sold out and was clearly another success.

'It became a hobby. We would see new namkeens in Bengali stores in Kolkata, buy some, bring them home, take them apart, and come up with our own versions that were way better than the local products,' said a satisfied Shiv Kishan. At seventy-five, he still grows animated at the memory of the 'good old days'. 'I know the individual tastes of every spice from cumin, cinnamon, pepper to cardamom and fennel. I can pinpoint the ingredients that go into most finished dishes,' he said in a matter-of-fact way that only he could pull off—humble, yet true. His personal secretary, Ankita, confirmed this on my visit to Nagpur: 'He tastes everything new we come up with and can straight away tell if something is missing, or if any ingredient could make the final product better. He has been tasting products, looking out for special ingredients all his life, but according to his stories, this skill got refined only in Kolkata.'

While everyone was great at making bhujia, Shiv Kishan had a special knack for recreating snacks that turned out better than the original. In an unspoken agreement, he spearheaded 'product innovation' in those days, even though they did not at the time have departments of any sort. Though the youngest at the time, not counting Rameshwarlal's own children who were all younger than ten, Shiv Kishan had quickly gained respect from the people who mattered the most to him—his grandfather and father.

In 1967, the shop in Kolkata was doing better than anybody had ever hoped. The profits were higher than they were in Bikaner, and Haldiram felt confident enough to leave his son Rameshwarlal in charge of the operations there. Haldiram gradually removed himself from the daily operations of the businesses, and frequently travelled between Bikaner and Kolkata to assist his sons in any way he could. It is said that he had the firm and gentle touch of a leader who could always hold the business and the family together.

However, trouble had been brewing between brothers Rameshwarlal and Satyanarayan—or as he was fondly called by family members, Sati Das—for a while. Perhaps it was a simple matter of two families finding it harder and harder to live under the same roof. As it had happened in the past, so it happened again. Sati Das chose to split from his father and brother Rameshwarlal, and started his own business in Kolkata under the name 'Haldiram & Sons'. Through some unspoken or rather unwritten, agreement, the business in Kolkata was divided, and Sati Das was provided with the funds necessary to start his own enterprise. Right then in the '60s began the first of the many familial challenges the Agarwal brothers would fight against in order to thrive. Bhujia competed against bhujia made from the same secret family recipe, while brother competed against brother for the same customers.

Haldiram Bhujiawala in Kolkata, then managed by Rameshwarlal, had an already established loyal customer base and flourishing business. While Haldiram & Sons offered some amount of competition, it only took away a handful of customers. The original business had such a strong foundation that it almost created an entry barrier for other similar firms, including the spin-off Haldiram & Sons, which struggled to garner enough of a clientele to pose any kind of threat to Rameshwarlal and Shiv Kishan. The initial days of the divide must have been stressful, as Rameshwarlal feared a loss in profits.

However, with the opening of the new Haldiram & Sons shop, a lot of the other snack shops in Kolkata began to sell their own versions of the bhujia. The family recipe was a closely guarded secret; however, as every great chef understands, practice makes perfect, and the various shopkeepers in Kolkata persevered to bring their bhujia up to standard. This created a sort of network externality effect. In network externalities, the more people that use a particular product, the more its value goes up, thereby bringing even more people on board. As more and more bhujia was available in the market, the more its demand grew and the cycle continued. The party most to benefit from this, ironically, was the original Haldiram Bhujiawala, as their product was clearly superior in taste and quality. Not only did this sudden surge in bhujia makers in Kolkata bring about a healthy dose of competition, it also increased the popularity of the snack, making it an important part of the customer's snack food ecosystem while also bringing more business to all shopkeepers.

## A Fissure Forms

From time immemorial, businesses have moved in order to set up new branches of operation on distant shores. Some business moves are completed to benefit from opportunities offered by a new land, such as the strategic migration of small film studios in 1910 from New Jersey to Los Angeles, California. These studios moved to take advantage of the fabulous weather in California, the large empty spaces to build their sets, increasing demand for feature films, especially westerns, and most importantly, the lack of unions in LA that gave them access to cheap labour. With this fateful move, the foundation for an entire industry was laid in a small town near Los Angeles, and Hollywood was born.

Other moves are made to support great ambitions of speedy expansion by migrating to economic centres, such as the one made by the south Indian fast-food chain Saravana Bhavan, when it crossed the Atlantic to set up shop in the US and London. Saravana Bhavan was trying to take advantage of the highly populated cosmopolitan parts in California, New York and London, hoping to quickly gain a share of the market. While there is intense competition in the various economic centres of the world, Saravana Bhavan was endeavouring to tap into the demand for quick, exotic meals in these cities by first wooing Indian followers and hoping to whet western appetites. Today they are one of the largest chains of Indian restaurants abroad.

Occasionally, however, moves are made without any strategic foresight, simply due to family pressure or pure serendipity, as was the case when Shiv Kishan moved to Nagpur. No matter the reasons behind a move, in every instance demand—whether existing or created—plays a vital role in the success of that business.

In 1968, all of Haldiram's three sons were settled, each managing a piece of the family's business—Moolchand looking after the shop in Bikaner, Rameshwarlal set up with Haldiram Bhujiawala in Kolkata and Satyanarayan managing a tiny piece of the business in the name of Haldiram & Sons, which eventually became independent from the businesses in Bikaner and Kolkata. Each nuclear family enjoyed stability, and more or less everyone was employed, making the most of the bhujia business. Moolchand's three younger sons were helping with the business in Bikaner and his oldest, Shiv Kishan was partnering with Rameshwarlal in the Haldiram Bhujiawala business in Kolkata. However, Moolchand's second child, a daughter named Saraswati Devi, had not been allowed to get her hands dirty in the family business, as was the tradition with girl children in Marwari communities. Saraswati Devi had been married when she was thirteen to a boy named Banshilal. While her ambitions had been great, her contributions to the family business had been almost nil, due to which she had not been included in the business family tree. While she has been inserted into the one for this book, it was impossible to find out the exact date and year of her birth. Ironically, Saraswati Devi indirectly played a major role in the family's expansion to Nagpur.

Saraswati Devi's husband, Banshilal, was a hard-working young man. He was a simpleton, a wheat-siever, who would repack sieved and cleaned wheat separated from the chaff in boris and sell these jute bags at local retail outlets. He was earning a modest income, but the labour was hard and the work would never ensure Saraswati Devi and her husband a life with any kind of comforts. 'She desperately wanted a part of the family business and begged our grandfather to set Banshilal up with a shop so they too could have a secure future,' said Shiv Kishan. He continued, 'Bikaner already had a business and it was being managed by an overkill of more than five people including my grandfather. It was therefore important to find another place to set up shop.' When asked why Nagpur, Shiv Kishan could come up with no reason at all. 'We chose Nagpur just like that,' he said. 'Why not Delhi?' On probing further, he said, 'I don't know. We didn't have any family or friends in Nagpur. Nor did we have an established community of Marwaris. Even though the city was not considered an economic hub at the time, my sister chose it as the place she wanted to live in, and we just went with it. As for Delhi, I guess we weren't ready at the time.'

In 1968, ten years after his marriage to Jamna Devi, Shiv Kishan was asked to go to Nagpur and help Saraswati Devi and her family set up the business there. He was originally supposed to go to Nagpur for a couple of weeks in March and handover the business to his sister and Banshilal, which he dutifully did.

What was initially planned as a short visit intended to show the newcomers the ropes, soon turned into a lifelong exile to this lacklustre town in Maharashtra.

No stranger to setting up shop and home in a new town, Shiv Kishan quickly found his sister and brother-in-law an apartment and rented a small shop on Post Office Road in the Itwari region of Nagpur. Strategically, Itwari was a business district with hundreds of workers who have been the primary segment that the Haldiram family has always targeted to kick-start sales.

Those two weeks in Nagpur were spent teaching Banshilal the art of making bhujia, and other basic snacks such as mixture and papadi, to get production going. 'The demand for snacks was not very high in Maharashtra and I reckoned that at a stable point, the business would be able to make on average ₹400 per day,' said Shiv Kishan. Satisfied that he had done what he could, he returned to resume his activities in Kolkata.

As luck would have it, six months into setting up at Nagpur, the business failed, and Saraswati Devi and Banshilal sent out an SOS, urgently requesting the family for help. While Shiv Kishan had taught them how to make the actual product, neither Banshilal nor his wife had any experience running a business or attracting customers. It was no surprise that they hardly made even 10 per cent of the expected daily sales, given that they made the bhujia and simply sat in their shop instead of actively reaching out to customers. Add to that, Maharashtrians were a very close-knit community, suspicious of outsiders and defensive of their local businesses.

This time, Shiv Kishan took his wife and children to Nagpur, knowing that it might take longer than he had originally expected to break even in this new business. 'I never had any intentions of settling down at Nagpur; however, familial duty beckoned,' he said. 'I gave myself three years at the outset, promising my wife that I would leave Nagpur after Diwali in 1971, so we could go back to Kolkata where we had friends and relatives, but fate had something else in store for us.'

While Shiv Kishan insists that the call of duty had forced his hand, a close family member shares another version of the events. In Kolkata, Shiv Kishan was living with Rameshwarlal and his wife, Kamala Devi. An assiduous young man, he was passionate about his work and usually worked late into the night. Many a time, he would be the last one to leave the shop, closing the counters and tallying the final numbers for the day. Kamala Devi, his aunt, would greet him at home, ensuring his dinner was served before he turned in for the night. It is rumoured that Kamala Devi was a tough woman with a very sharp tongue, but more importantly, she was very suspicious of him, most times without reason. She would ask him to empty his pockets to ensure he hadn't taken any money for himself from the counter, in spite of his vehement declarations of honesty. Allegedly, a deeply disturbed Shiv Kishan had finally found the nerve to telephone his father and share his grievances with him. It was then that Moolchand and Haldiram created a job for him in Nagpur to take him away for a short period, giving everybody in Kolkata some breathing space.

Even though time heals all wounds, a couple of weeks that Shiv Kishan initially spent in Nagpur were not enough to change attitudes. The close family member also reveals that at a family gathering a few months later, Kamala Devi snidely said something along the lines of, 'You have a wonderful life! You have absolutely nothing to worry about. The Kolkata business is doing great, and you simply have to sit around and enjoy the fruits of our labour.' The remark landed exactly where it was meant to, and a proud and enraged Shiv Kishan gladly accepted the second Nagpur assignment. It is said that Moolchand, in a typical Bollywood-father fashion, told his son not to show his face to the family till he was standing on his own two feet!

Although Shiv Kishan himself did not mention this story, the interviews about his days in Kolkata and the twenty-four-year-old brand battle were underlined by a barely concealed animosity towards his uncle and his family. Answers were interlaced with words such as 'greed' and 'bad seed' relaying his feelings towards that family.

It is said that Shiv Kishan discovered his true mettle in the days leading up to his departure from Kolkata that later fuelled the very flames that inspired him to build his empire in Nagpur. Hurt pride proved to be a great catalyst for inspiration, and inspiration led to the virtuous cycle of passion generating positive action. Shiv Kishan found his heart burning with ambition leading to not just his conquering Nagpur but setting the wheels in motion for the family to finally expand to the capital as well. It is sad that while it was he who strategized the move to Delhi, he never got to play a major role in growing the business there. However, his successes in Nagpur helped lay the foundation for expansion across the country.

The move to Nagpur was also significant in that it was the first sign of minor rifts between Moolchand's and Rameshwarlal's families. When Shiv Kishan moved to Nagpur and eventually took over the business there, Rameshwarlal and his sons were almost singularly dominating Kolkata. In a way, both of theirs were the only nuclear family units in this patriarchal joint-family system. This minor separation and weakening of ties ultimately lead to a multi-year battle, publically bleeding both sides of the family of their resources, dignity and inheritance.

Once again, the narrative follows personal insults into the boardroom, forging a strong theme in the story of the Agarwals, where betrayed trust led to splintering the family and the business, restricting it and its founders from realizing their true potential.

## The Orange City

The second trip to Nagpur was different. This time, Shiv Kishan had greater stake in the business and also had much to prove to himself as well as to his father. He handpicked a few karigars, or craftsmen, and took them with him to Nagpur. Instead of immediately deploying the workforce and jumping into making what he knew best how to make, Shiv Kishan adopted a more studied approach, a definite step up from the family's usual practice. At thirty, though still young, Shiv Kishan had already been through the struggle of starting out in a brand new town, had identified his own special talents, aka tasting for ingredients and developing new products, and had, above all, discovered a sense of purpose. He not only wanted to set up shop in the new city, he wanted to do it better than anybody in his family had done before.

Breaking the mould, Shiv Kishan decided to start with surveying the market and assessing the competition. He visited Mishthan Bhandar & Dorabjee, among other popular shops and restaurants in Nagpur, to gauge the palate of the Maharashtrians as well as the demand in the market. Very quickly he realized that Maharashtrians had not yet been exposed to more than a few savoury snacks, which presented him with a huge opportunity to be a first mover in the market; he was sure that the locals would take to the snacks he was so good at making. He was hoping to replicate the success they had had with the Bengalis. The second gap he identified was in the sweets market. The popular shops mostly sold *balusha*s, Gujarati *peda*s, Mysore *pak* and laddus. This told the young entrepreneur two things: Maharashtrians definitely had a sweet tooth that could be exploited further, and there were hundreds of sweet delicacies from other regions that could be leveraged for market penetration.

He followed the old adage of doing what the Romans did in Rome and decided to start with making sweets and winning the customers over with what they already liked, before trying to introduce their palates to completely new flavours. Shiv Kishan had always secretly wanted to diversify the product line into sweets, he confessed during our interview in Nagpur. He was forever experimenting with sweets even when he was in Kolkata but always bowed to his uncle Rameshwarlal's better judgement. Rameshwarlal and his father, Moolchand, were both made of the same old cloth, believing that the business should stick to producing what it was good at. While this helped the family maintain and even strengthen their core value offering, it would have ultimately limited their growth and made them vulnerable to predatory competitors who were forever trying to copy the original Haldiram bhujia recipe.

Marwari families have stood strong for centuries on the bedrock of their established traditions, the most important being deference to elders. Seniority has always equalled wisdom for this community—breaking this hierarchy is almost considered an unspoken form of heresy. This trend becomes more pronounced in later chapters through the struggles of the heirs of the respective business units right up until the twenty-first century. If Haldiram gave an order, everyone in the household would simply hold their opinions, swallow hard, and follow his edict. This 'seniority effect' has been passed down from father to son for generations and has triggered a degree of rebellion within each passing generation, marking the success of the business over time. However, it was indeed ironic that each of the Agarwal men at some point in their lives challenged this authority, carving out their own individual paths, starting with Haldiram himself where he set the precedent by breaking away from his grandfather and brothers in 1944. While Shiv Kishan was in Kolkata, it was near impossible for him to break the chain of command and begin diversifying the product line. Even if he could have finally convinced the elders, it might not have happened for years to come or, worse yet, he might have missed the opportunity by staying silent in an attempt to not disrespect his elders by going against their wishes. And Marwaris take respect very seriously.

As luck would have it, in 1968 in Nagpur, Shiv Kishan was suddenly his own master. He was responsible for all operational decisions and this newfound freedom gave him all the encouragement he needed to set his ideas in motion. He started by making his favourite sweet, today's popular *kaju katli*. It is usually prepared by thickening milk with sugar, dry fruits, mainly cashew nuts, and saffron. Kaju katli is now one of the most expensive sweets in the market and is a rich delicacy that is gifted by friends and families during festivals and special occasions. Adopting the sampling and food-tasting promotions he had witnessed in Kolkata, Shiv Kishan launched the kaju katli in Nagpur. As the word of mouth spread, the sweet began to gain popularity. 'It first started with people buying 100 g and then 200 g and then gradually 500 g. The flavour was accepted and loved and soon we were flooded with demands for kaju katli,' said Shiv Kishan.

Excited by the successful launch of his first sweet product, Shiv Kishan began to flesh out the entire category with relish, thus commencing the brand's journey of becoming one of the largest players in the sweets industry. He introduced the locals to delights from Bikaner and Kolkata, especially *malai* laddu, rasgulla and ras malai, and his customers could not get enough of the Haldiram Bhujiawala sweets.

Within three years, the business was flourishing. Shiv Kishan had added another branch to the business in Sai Chowk, and customer recognition for the brand was steadily growing. 'When we started, we were making on average ₹100 a day, but within three years, our sales had gone up to ₹500 a day, nearly increasing our revenues by a whopping 400 per cent!' said Shiv Kishan. This might seem like a meagre amount today, but for a small-time businessman in the '70s, it was a huge victory. To put things in perspective, a kilo of sugar that could have been purchased for ₹2 in the '70s, now costs ₹40. To further exemplify, a government servant, after approximately ten years of service earned an annual salary of ₹5000 in the 1970s. This amount, once broken down into monthly payments comes to ₹417 before taxes. In comparison, Shiv Kishan's revenues were ₹15,000 per month. Now, while government servants were considered lower-middle class in those days, Shiv Kishan was by no means an upper-middle class citizen based on his earnings. He was, however, an entrepreneur, making decent profits and making his way up in the world.

In addition to taking on all responsibilities in Nagpur, he also took Banshilal under his wing. Shiv Kishan shared all the family secrets and endeavoured to cultivate a businesslike shrewdness in his brother-in-law but alas, it was all in vain. Not only was Banshilal poor at making the actual products, he also didn't have the right instincts when it came to customers. 'It embarrasses me to admit it, but Banshilal simply couldn't make it like we did. He also somehow did not have the understanding required to create the right hospitable environment for customers. Nonetheless, he was a hard worker and I was determined to have him in the saddle before my Diwali deadline of 1971,' said Shiv Kishan. He added ruefully, 'Life, however, doesn't always go as planned.' Before Shiv Kishan could pack up and leave, tragedy left the Agarwal household reeling in shock.

Electrical voltage fluctuations are a common phenomenon in India, especially so in the early decades after independence. That, combined with the fact that high-power electrical devices such as elevators, air conditioners and refrigerators require a lot of energy to switch on and off, components like compressors and motors create sudden, brief demands for power. These surges can be severe enough to damage the components by gradually making the devices themselves dangerous and capable of producing high-voltage shocks that can be fatal to a human being. Banshilal was found lying on the floor of their shop following one such terrible accident. It is said that he died instantly after having received a high-voltage jolt from the refrigerator, but nobody can be sure.

In the days following her husband's death, Saraswati Devi lost all desire to carry on with life. In a single brutal instant, she had been left lost and grieving, her sense of family dissolved. She would spend most of her time staring listlessly into space. 'She was morose and upset, and lost all interest in the business. Realizing that she needed a change in scenery, we suggested that she visit Bikaner for a break,' said Shiv Kishan. 'Once she went to Bikaner, my father realized that a mere change in scenery would not be enough. What she really needed was time. At that point, he ordered me to stay back and manage the business. Something told me it would be permanent this time.'

An already ambitious Shiv Kishan was beginning to sense that Nagpur might actually end up being his legacy, after all. With renewed enthusiasm and focus, he looked into growth opportunities and possible avenues the business could pursue. Now he was not just working as hard as usual but pushing himself harder, spending more hours at the shop and all the while evaluating his business. It seems he was drowning his sorrows in his work and the sudden responsibility of ownership had given him a renewed sense of energy. The added business obligations after Banshilal's death helped Shiv Kishan channel his energies into the next big foray for the business—the restaurant space.

'I happened to visit this restaurant called Kirti and it was an eye-opener. They had a very limited menu, specializing in dosa and lassi. They were attracting considerable crowds and I was inspired. I thought to myself, if they can do it, I can do it better!' said Shiv Kishan. 'Surveying the market, we realized that south Indian snacks such as dosa and idli were extremely popular in Nagpur.' While eager to introduce Maharashtrians to delicacies from Bikaner, Shiv Kishan took the long route of starting with items that had the greatest current demand. He opened a restaurant that could seat approximately thirty people, adjacent to the shop in Sai Chowk. 'Our first menu had idli and dosa, and I can tell you we posed serious competition to the local restaurants serving the same!' said Shiv Kishan with a chuckle. It is always amazing to see someone succeed at something they had not grown up doing. For instance, an Italian succeeding at establishing an Asian restaurant!

The restaurant was soon filled with noise and chatter, and with every seat taken, they very quickly had to expand its capacity. They went from serving dosa and idlis to what they were truly good at—samosas and kachoris. The business continued to grow, but with fame also came envy from neighbours. Like most young entrepreneurs without a benefactor, the path to success was not a smooth one for Shiv Kishan.

Seeking solace in familiarity, Shiv Kishan had found Nagpur's extreme weather and small-town feel an initial comfort before being faced with the challenge of expanding the business in a hostile locality, sans the support of a close-knit community or knowledge of local customs and languages.

His early successes had not prepared for him for the crisis that followed.

For months after opening his first restaurant, Shiv Kishan faced hooligans who refused to pay after ordering food, threatening his staff and resorting to vandalism. The gangsters even deterred customers from entering the premises. Shiv Kishan's staff was terribly intimidated by them, especially since some of them carried menacing knives and bicycle chains as part of their arsenal. When asked why the staff did not take a firmer stance, Shiv Kishan revealed that one of the hooligans was the son of the then deputy mayor of Nagpur. These tactics were meant to scare our young entrepreneur off, but the Agarwals do not retreat without a fight.

Staging a war against a corrupt politician is projected as probably the single most challenging task in Bollywood films. And as they say, there is no smoke without a fire! It is definitely one of the greatest trials of being an ordinary citizen in India, especially since many corrupt coppers are in the pockets of politicians. Shiv Kishan, however, developed a friendship with a police officer, Inspector Ajij, who was both honest and strong of will.

One evening, the group of troublemakers arrived at the shop and ordered tea and goodies. One of them plucked a strand of hair and dropped it in the tea when he thought nobody was looking, but a waiter in the shop noticed. The hooligan created a huge hue and cry about the unhygienic conditions of the restaurant and the chef's complete disregard for the customer's health and well-being. He refused to pay for any of the items on the bill and began to throw verbal insults at the staff, scaring other customers in the restaurant. Bursting with fury, Shiv

Kishan called Inspector Ajij and complained. 'I then stood my ground and refused to let them leave without paying the bill,' he said with dramatic flair.

'But what if they had turned violent and hurt you?' was the obvious question that followed. To which he said, a twinkle in his eye, 'In my youth, I was much stronger than I seem now. I was crazy about being strong. My friends and I would lift weights all the time. I would carry oil cans in each arm and we would clock the time it took before we gave up in agony and threw the can down. Each can weighed about thirty kilos!'

Strong and confident, Shiv Kishan held his ground by forming a line with his employees to block the hoodlums till the inspector arrived. Inspector Ajij, true to his reputation, arrested the deputy mayor's son without a second's hesitation in spite of knowing the risk he was taking. There must have been immense pressure from above but the good inspector did not cave in and held the boy for three days to teach him about the consequences of his actions. 'The message was sent,' said Shiv Kishan in a quiet voice. The local community learnt not to mess with him and began to know him as the businessman with 'connections'. 'Sai Chowk then became my home. People respected me and thanks to Inspector Ajij, there was peace in our outlets,' said Shiv Kishan.

The Haldiram Bhujiawala brand's popularity continued to grow and Shiv Kishan's outlets soon became some of the most visited shops for snacks and sweets as well as fast-food meals in Nagpur. 'I began dreaming big. I wanted to rule the snacks and sweets industry in Nagpur, but then I thought of capturing the nation's capital. Delhi became almost an obsession and I could not get it out of my mind,' said Shiv Kishan. With

each achievement in Nagpur, Shiv Kishan grew even more
determined and confident that he could set up shop in Delhi and
become a competitive player in that market. Shiv Kishan then
began sharing his plans with his younger brother, Manoharlal,
back in Bikaner.

In 1977, the demand was incessant and Shiv Kishan started
a shop in Dharampeth in Nagpur, followed closely by the
opening of another outlet in Badi in 1980. In the meantime,
Saraswati Devi had returned to stay in Nagpur while her dutiful
brother continued to grow the business. It was only a matter of
time before she realized that Shiv Kishan had begun a legacy
that would one day be bequeathed to his sons. Without an
active part in the business, in her bid to be protective of her
family, she nurtured feelings of jealousy and insecurity that her
son might never be allowed to play a vital part in the business's
growth. She had one son and two daughters and with her
husband not around, she felt the need to pass down something
concrete. It never occurred to her to stay unified after the huge
demonstration of love and duty that Shiv Kishan had shown by
uprooting his family, moving to Nagpur and looking after the
business so that his sister could fulfil her dream of being a part
of the family's legacy.

In the same year that Shiv Kishan launched the outlet in
Badi, Saraswati Devi made her demands. She wanted a portion
of the business for her children and spoke to her father and
grandfather about what she called a 'reasonable inheritance'.
While Marwari families are usually conservative, and women
have always been considered secondary to business, Moolchand
Agarwal, who was very fond of his daughter, agreed to her terms
and the business was split as soon as the demand was made.

'My father demanded that the Sai Chowk shop and restaurant be given to her along with a sum of money to set her children up, and I did,' Shiv Kishan corroborated. This is yet another example of the respect sons had for their fathers and the strong deference to hierarchy within Marwari families. Even as grown men and head honchos, they were always subject to the higher edict and wisdom of their fathers and grandfathers. What is interesting to note is that even in the twentieth century, Shiv Kishan and his brothers felt compelled to follow convention and accede to their elders.

Most splits within the business have been resolved quietly, under the table, such as this one. Verbal promises between family members have been considered binding, thereby helping the family avoid legal headaches. By 1980, the family was spread across Bikaner, Kolkata and Nagpur and yet, they had not even begun thinking about a formalized succession plan and legal contracts to protect them in the future. Shiv Kishan was a part of the third generation of Haldiram's lineage and had till that point never truly seen a major division in the business and the family. Mutually accepted verbal agreements were still a safe form of splitting the business in his mind.

In spite of having to give away one of his biggest outlets, Shiv Kishan and family were flourishing in Nagpur. Business was soaring, generating new product lines and innovations, which in turn were driving sales further upwards. By 1980, they had four outlets in Nagpur, with another one on its way. Shiv Kishan would share his profits with his father and brothers back home in Bikaner. While Nagpur was doing well, Bikaner was far behind in the race for revenues and growth. Conversely, Kolkata was at that time their biggest operation. The Kolkata unit was making the highest profits and was also profit-sharing with Bikaner.

The funny part in all of this is that while Bikaner, the family headquarters, was receiving a share of Kolkata's and Nagpur's profits and Nagpur was receiving a cut from Kolkata, Kolkata was receiving nothing from Nagpur. This is how the seniority and hierarchy came into play. The sons always paid the father his due and so it was with the Haldiram family. Since profits generated from the Bikaner business were peanuts, Kolkata, in a way, was not receiving much from any direction. It was only a matter of time before discontentment leaked its way into the existing harmony. Around 1975, Rameshwarlal from Kolkata began to drop hints to Moolchand in Bikaner along the lines of, 'My children are young and none of them can help me at the business for many more years to come. I am overwhelmed with work and responsibility and would appreciate it if you could spare someone to help with my business in Kolkata.'

Sensitive and intuitive, Moolchand realized what his brother truly desired. A close relative confirms, 'Moolchand sensed his brother's discontent. He knew that when Rameshwarlal asked him to send one of his sons to Kolkata, it was intended to let him know that while profits were being shared, the work was not! Moolchand immediately asked his brother if he wished to separate, and Rameshwarlal and his wife, Kamala Devi, jumped at the opportunity. It was agreed that they would give each other what they owed in terms of their shares in each other's businesses and separate amicably.' It was also agreed that Haldiram, Moolchand and Shiv Kishan would not enter West Bengal, which would remain Rameshwarlal's territory, beginning the 'territory distribution system' unique to the Haldiram family in the twenty-first century.

While family ties continued to remain amicable, the business separation itself was steeped in the base human emotions of pride and envy. Passions and sentiments came in the way of business. This could have been the perfect opportunity for fair play, with Shiv Kishan offering to share profits with the Kolkata unit as well. However, he also felt justified in his sense of pride in his set-up and his sense of possessiveness that emerged from having built something from the ground up. His past experience with Rameshwarlal and Kamala Devi might have led him to harbour feelings of righteous anger. In the current day, Shiv Kishan's brother Manoharlal implied that the demand for change came from Kolkata and implicitly indicated that ambition fuelled his uncle's desire to separate.

Shiv Kishan and Manoharlal, part of the third generation of the Haldiram clan, are today witnessing a bitter battle with their Kolkata cousins. The seeds of the battle were sowed by the generation before them; however, it is the way of the world for sons to fight their fathers' wars. 'Only 15 per cent of family businesses make it past the third generation,' touts the *Wall Street Journal*. Most globally reckoned with family enterprises such as Johnson & Johnson and the Mayo Clinic only survived the test of time because they realized early on to develop robust policies and processes to manage succession and the involvement of human ties and emotions in business. This alone possibly forms the foundation for the multibillion-dollar enterprises to have thrived and succeeded over decades.

The separation of Rameshwarlal from Moolchand and Haldiram in terms of profit-sharing triggered an era of each owner managing their own business with no interference from others, as if their business unit was a separate company in its own right. While this trend propelled each brother to want to possess his own unit, thereby breaking up the whole into more fragmented pieces, it also fulfilled their need to be independent and assuaged their individual ambitions. Whether the individual units are stronger on their own is yet to be ascertained.

More autonomous after the business ties with Kolkata were severed, Shiv Kishan felt especially compelled to expand to the capital. Perhaps he was finally attaining the confidence to make the 'big' move, or perchance a rebellious move on his part as he was no longer allowed to set up business in Kolkata. Yet, the move to Delhi proved momentous to the success of the business and flung the brand into the national and global spotlights.

# PART III

# THE CAPITAL

# Glimpses of Glamour

'Delhi was my ambition,' said Shiv Kishan.

Proud, ambitious and determined, Shiv Kishan dreamed of conquering the capital. He believed that with their quality products and immensely popular flavours and textures, they could capture the capital in no time. However, Shiv Kishan was a family man, and being a part of the family business, he was obliged to first set up and take care of the shop in Nagpur. Once his brother-in-law had passed away, the weight of the business fell to him and he took on the responsibility with no complaints.

With each passing year, the business in Nagpur grew and so did his desire to expand. However, while Nagpur had begun to do well, it was not in league with the Kolkata business, especially given that Kolkata in those days was a centre of commerce. While the profits grew, he did not yet have the margins or the savings to build a business from ground up in the Rajdhani. Toiling upwards into the night in Nagpur, he kept the flame of his dream to move to Delhi alive, waiting for the right moment, the right time.

In the late '70s, his younger brother Manoharlal, then in his early twenties, was beginning to show a spark that Shiv Kishan hadn't seen in his other siblings yet. Younger to Shiv Kishan by about fifteen years, Manoharlal was just beginning to learn about the business in Bikaner under the guidance of his father,

Moolchand, and his grandfather, Haldiram, when his older brother was making great strides in Nagpur.

At family meetings, get-togethers and holidays, the two brothers, in spite of their huge age gap, began to form a strong bond of camaraderie and friendship. They planned and plotted and together began forging a path towards Delhi. While Shiv Kishan was the spark that ignited the flame of ambition, it was Manoharlal who took the idea and ran with it, establishing the brand in Delhi with great initiative, creativity and remarkable style.

Shiv Kishan and his brothers in the years that followed divided the family business in a unique territory-based agreement where they do not infringe upon each other's regions. Today, Shiv Kishan, the eldest, is the owner of the Nagpur business units and the pioneer behind Delhi. The second brother is Shiv Ratan who owns Bikaji in Bikaner. Next comes Manoharlal, the owner of Haldiram's in Delhi, followed by his youngest brother and partner, Madhusudan.

\* \* \*

# Delhi Diaries

The journey to Bikaner, Nagpur and Kolkata brought history to life, sparking a deeper sense of admiration for the family's humble roots, the drive and voracity with which they have pursued success and their utter devotion to quality both in product and customer service. Each city, hot in its own unique way, was conquered with courage, faith and steady determination.

What was interesting to find were the dichotomies within their very human personalities. The heroes, at times, were tainted in shades of grey, and the rogues occasionally bathed in white rays. The family itself served as a sturdy foundation for the business, yet through the ages has also been one of its greatest weaknesses.

Bikaner, Nagpur and Kolkata laid the foundation for the brand's extraordinary story, laced in sweat and tears, but it was Delhi that gave it a voice to reckon with. Haldiram, Shiv Kishan and Rameshwarlal were all hard-working, ambitious men, perhaps even visionaries to the extent their capabilities allowed, but it was Moolchand's younger son Manoharlal who had both the means and the unrelenting fire required to break the mould and set the course for global recognition.

Driving through the labyrinthine roads of Noida, I was expecting to find the usual two-storeyed building, covered with dust, based on my previous experiences in Bikaner, Nagpur and Kolkata. By then, I had learnt that these men believed in growing wealth but not in being ostentatious. While most of their offices had been tastefully decorated, I never got a sense of status, prestige or 'corporate' during my visits. Stopping at the gates of the corporate offices of Haldiram's in Sector 62 in Noida, I couldn't help but gasp at the glorious metal-and-glass structure in front of me. A five-storeyed structure, here was finally physical evidence of the success I had been pursuing.

Walking into the reception, I was greeted by modern furniture in elegant hues, and brightening the room were a few select paintings and vases. The receptionist, professional and friendly, led me to wait in a state-of-the-art meeting room with double-shaded glass walls granting privacy, yet allowing the inmates of the room a wide view of the office floor beyond.

There was activity all around—employees holding files in discussion with one another were perched on desks and chairs, peons were rushing around with important messages, phones were ringing, and yet there was a sense of discipline and decorum in the chaos. The room itself was fitted with videoconferencing facilities. Drinking my tea, I was wondering how open these Delhiites would be to my questioning and prodding. The folks at Bikaner and Nagpur had exhibited an innocence of media, an innocence I had vowed I would not take advantage of. They had invited me into their homes and shared their stories as if I were a relative stopping by for a little respite and needing reminders of the families' many adventures before I went on my way. I knew that a greater degree of organization, while good for a company, also led to caginess, and I hoped that I could tell this story in all its glory.

After a few interviews with key staff, I was invited Manoharlal's penthouse suite. Waiting in the swanky reception area, I bumped into Pramod Tapadia, one of Manoharlal's oldest friends and colleagues. Surprised by his warmth and friendliness, we got chatting. It seems the two friends ate dinner together almost every evening. Tapadia would finish his work for the day and meet Manoharlal at his office, where they would discuss business and life, as Manoharlal's staff served them a healthy and delicious meal.

'The building was just constructed a few months ago,' said Tapadia, as I commented on the plush decor of the office. It was indeed beautiful and tastefully decorated.

'I was the first to congratulate him when he sat in his office here,' said Tapadia. 'You've come so far, I told him and Manoharlal replied, "You helped carry me here."'

I had heard tales of Manoharlal's humility and the finesse with which he commanded the loyalty of so many workers, colleagues and contemporaries. Tapadia's comment was another such anecdote in my arsenal, but I was eager to see it for myself.

Short and rotund like his brothers; the sixty-year-old Manoharlal greeted me with a broad smile on his face, apologizing for the delay. Once seated, he asked softly, 'What can I tell you that my brothers haven't already?' There was a deference in his tone, and I realized here was a man who had set up an empire in the capital and yet praised his brothers as more knowledgeable about the business. Before he could help himself, another question almost immediately followed the first. Genuinely curious, 'You are writing a book about us?' he asked incredulously, pausing as if in deep thought and then again, 'Why us? Why not Balaji or some other brand that came into the market in the last decade or so and took everyone by surprise?'

Thus began the hours of interviewing at Delhi. With each passing minute, he grew more comfortable and recounted tales of such adventure that I could only wonder at the courage and sheer guts that he had displayed. His stories spoke of rebellion, of trying to do the right thing, of facing the consequences of ones choices, all regaled with the cheerful humorous air of one who has truly experienced the challenges of life and learnt to laugh at them.

\* \* \*

The Gayatri Maha Mantram played softly in the backdrop adding to the relaxed atmosphere. At 8.30 p.m., Manoharlal sat

behind his desk quickly looking through important documents
and issues that needed immediate attention before turning to
me. Tapadia sat patiently waiting for his friend to finish his work
while the peon came in with fresh fruit and a simple dinner of
*fulkas* and vegetables. The two friends, Manoharlal and Tapadia,
shared such a meal on a daily basis and I had been invited to be
a part of the ritual. Just before we got started, his wife called
to check whether he had taken his medications and was eating
dinner, to which he gently responded with reassurances, an
indication of a caring relationship between the two. It made
me smile.

'It all began with Shiv Kishan,' he said. 'He dreamed of
moving the business to Delhi. We would talk about it on the
phone and discuss the move at length. Kolkata had gone into
our uncle's share, and our father refused to allow Shiv Kishan
to set up shop there since a family member had already begun
business in the eastern city. Having successfully grown a business
in Nagpur, Shiv Kishan was even more impatient to move to the
capital. I was simply the vehicle to help move and manage the
business, it was Shiv Kishan's dream that gave us the impetus
we needed.'

They inaugurated their first shop in Delhi at Chandni
Chowk in February 1983. When Manoharlal arrived there in
the latter half of 1982, Chandni Chowk was known for famous
snack vendors like Ghantewala, Kanwarlalji, Chainaram
Sindhi, Annapurna as well as Bikanervala. 'We had never seen
so much competition. Each brand had its own loyal following
of customers, and demand in Delhi was a phenomenon we had
not yet experienced,' said Manoharlal. 'Yet, the market was huge
and we realized quite quickly that there was more than enough

room for us and our products!' All of Delhi's top restaurants at the time were in Chandni Chowk, and excelling in the capital required great grit, expertise and shrewdness on their part.

According to Manoharlal, it had all happened through a combination of hard work, dedication and God's grace as he recalled the journey from the very beginning. The brothers, Shiv Kishan and Manoharlal, bought a space in '82, and by '83 Manoharlal and Madhusudan had built and fitted a workshop with everything they would require to conduct business. Within a year, they were breaking even and building a reputation of quality for themselves. Then devastation struck in the form of the 1984 Sikh riots. The Sikh baker's shop below their two storeys was burnt to the ground and with that their home, shop and livelihood.

Everything that they had worked hard for and struggled to build was destroyed within moments in the fire.

'Fear was natural, as was disbelief. It was not so much the fire, but the realization that most of our home and factory had been scorched to the ground. There was a terrible sinking feeling in the heart as we watched our future burn down right in front of us,' recalled Manoharlal.

In 1984, following Operation Blue Star, when Indira Gandhi had ordered the army to flush terrorists out from the sacred Golden Temple in Amritsar, she was assassinated by two Sikh soldiers on 31 October. Chaos followed her assassination with crowds of people taking to the streets pledging vengeance on all Sikhs. As violence broke out, the lives of the residents of Chandni Chowk, one of the most crowded areas in the city, were in danger. A curfew was imposed, barring residents from being out on the streets after sundown. The curfew lasted for at least a week after the assassination and a lot of businesses in Chandni Chowk suffered, including the small Haldiram shop in the heart of the market.

While Manoharlal's home and factory on the two floors above their home were decimated, the shop thankfully was left unscathed. However, due to the curfew none of their stocked product could be sold for a week after the assassination. For a small-time business that relies on daily sales to feed their family, this was a huge hit. Manoharlal, Madhusudan and their families found a small hotel nearby to stay for a few days. The men stayed on to work through the challenges, while the women and children were sent back to Bikaner out of safety concerns as well as financial ones.

Capital was dwindling. With help and support from the Bikaner and Nagpur branches, Moolchand's youngest sons bought another workshop space of about 300–400 sq. ft close to their previous quarters in Chandni Chowk. Their first shop was eight-by-eleven feet in area and the factory space neatly complimented the shop in terms of production.

It took them a couple of months following the crisis to repair and rebuild their home. The brothers ran double shifts in this new factory in order to up production and make up for the losses in the fire. They moved the karigars from the old workshop space to the new one, assigning shifts to their workers. The night shift focused on building their reservoir of sweets, and then during the day, they made namkeens. Over the next few months, the brothers built two more floors above the initial 300 sq. ft, giving them a total of 600 sq. ft of production space. 'Once our building was repaired, we had two workshops running at the same time. The new space was dedicated to sweet production and our original workshop continued to manufacture namkeens,' said Manoharlal.

Slowly and steadily Manoharlal recovered from the setback, fired by a fresh spark of ambition kindling in his belly. Success was suddenly a necessity, not a dream. The fire had challenged his ability to survive, and somewhere along the way, he had made it his personal mission to take the brand where nobody else before him had.

Delhi could have been a challenge for even a veteran businessman. So what prepared a twenty-eight-year-old novice for this feat? What was Manoharlal's journey like before entering the capital?

## The Boy Who Wouldn't Listen

Manoharlal Agarwal was born on 30 October 1954, just a couple of years before his grandfather and uncle Rameshwarlal journeyed to Kolkata. While his elder brother Shiv Kishan was out making his mark in Kolkata, the toddler Manoharlal was having a whale of a time growing up. Unlike his entire family before him, Manoharlal enjoyed a real childhood. He experienced the joys of leisure and retained his youthful innocence a while longer without the responsibilities of the business and a family weighing him down.

An academic at heart, his education did not end when he passed the eighth grade from Agrasen School, instead he went on to complete his schooling from Jain school and also did his BCom from Jain College. He was the first and only graduate of the whole family up until the next generation when his children also pursued higher education. While exposed to the family business, Manoharlal for a long time was not sure if he would join it. In 1973, he graduated from BCom in Bikaner and informed his father that he did not have any desire to join the family business. Moolchand, for his part, demonstrated great restraint and open-mindedness for those times when he permitted his son to decide the course of his life for himself instead of pressurizing him to join the business, as was the norm in business families. This was perhaps one of the only moments where father and son saw eye-to-eye on any matter for years to come. Moolchand was perhaps reminded of his own youth when his heart had never been in the business, yet fate and duty had pulled him into its folds.

With his father's blessings, young Manoharlal went to Kolkata to pursue further education in chartered accounting. Within six months, he realized the vast difference between the life of a businessman and a professional. He realized how much harder he would have to work to make it in the world without a launch pad. He also realized his own potential as an accountant and creative thinker and the asset that he could be to the family business. The business was already set up; all he had to do was apply all his comparatively excessive education and creative energy to improving it and making it better than ever before. Now a young man with a firm purpose, it was easier for him to quit college and head back home to work in the business than it would have been if he hadn't known what his mission was.

In 1975, the storefront in Bikaner, set up by Haldiram, was a small shop. 'We produced five hundred to six hundred kilos of bhujia a month, and our profit margin was much lower than that of Kolkata as we couldn't raise the price of the end product given how small Bikaner's economy was,' said Manoharlal.

Moolchand had disliked working in production or behind the scenes simply because it was unpleasant grunt work. However, unlike his father, Manoharlal was a man of action. He couldn't bear sitting in the shop, talking to customers while all that precious time could be spent actually improving the business. Once on the path, the young padawan took his charge very seriously. 'I spent most of my waking hours in the workshop. At six in the morning, I would be at the workshop, sans a shower or breakfast,' said Manoharlal. At my slight grimace, he smiled and added, 'I would freshen up first!'

The workshop was next door to their house. Manoharlal was keen to observe and learn the processes before jumping in with both feet. With help from the karigars, he began by completely understanding the product. Highly interested in its formulation, he would spend hours experimenting, tasting and manipulating the bhujia. In his early days in the business, Manoharlal noticed discrepancies in how the product was weighed and packaged for the customer. He realized that each pack they sold was of a slightly different weight, and over dozens of packs and kilos, the shop was taking a loss because of these inconsistencies.

'I always wanted to reduce inconsistencies in the making of the batches and also improve processes. My aim was to streamline the business to reduce variations and ultimately costs,' he said. His knowledge of accounting spurred him to want to increase profits and he clearly had an eye for major cost centres. However, at no point had he been exposed to the concept of Henry Ford's production line or to process improvements at Toyota to understand the impact these tiny changes would have on the overall efficiency and success of the business. Yet, this twenty-one-year-old pursued these ideas with a fervour regardless of the opposition from his elders to ensure that both the Haldiram product and brand would be standardized, primed to someday enjoy economies of scale.

Hurt pride and indignation can at times be great facilitators. In combination with his new-found purpose to improve the family business, Manoharlal was further spurred on by the desire to be better than the rest. The original shop, owned by Haldiram's grandfather, Bhikharam Chandmal, was right across the road from Haldiram's shop. One fine day, while working in his shop, Manoharlal overheard some customers mention that Bhikharam Chandmal's bhujia was better than Haldiram's.

'I was deeply disturbed. I hated to be thought of as mediocre or second best. I never liked it when our product fared below par when compared to another. I wanted our brand, our product, to be 110 per cent better than anybody else's,' said Manoharlal, his eyes flashing. Even after all these years, at sixty, the memory stood out for him like a sore thumb. Manoharlal's blood boiled when customers drew such comparisons, urging him to innovate and further develop the business, demonstrating his innate competitiveness and passion to be better than anybody else. A college-educated Marwari, a businessman, an achiever, Manoharlal was well on his way to discovering himself and his true potential.

Doubly focused on improving the product, Manoharlal set out in earnest to understand the differences between all the products in the market, while adding and removing ingredients to achieve better taste and quality. He discovered that adding cloves to bhujia made it even more delicious. With confirmation from customers who indeed found the new bhujia delectable, Manoharlal added the ingredient to the recipe. However, cloves were much more expensive than regular spices, affecting their already slim margins. 'My father, who was extremely conservative about change of any sort, would ask enraged, "How will we live with such margins?"' Manoharlal related with a guffaw. Moolchand resisted new ideas with the force of a man who was completely comfortable within set parameters and stable routines. He was a man of habit, and any change would shake him up, sending father and son spiralling into long arguments. 'I bought myself time by telling him to wait and see, and if it didn't work, we would revert back to the old ways,' said Manoharlal, exhibiting a sensitivity in dealing with people and an understanding that diplomacy and tact could win over even the hardest of customers. People took to the new bhujia enthusiastically and the shop saw greater sales offsetting the slight dip in margins per pack.

To improve product quality, it is important to minutely monitor the actual raw material that goes into the product. One of the key ingredients for a type of bhujia was besan. Besan for the bhujia was purchased in heaps, pre-ground to a fine powder. A couple of workers had bought a small flour mill and set themselves up near the shop, a testament to the simplicity of those times. At that time, Haldiram and his son did not even own a grinder. They would buy the besan and directly use it in the preparation of their products. 'We couldn't even tell if it was adulterated or whether it was of good quality. We simply bought it because that was the way it had been done for years,' related Manoharlal. Later, it would become regular practice to buy the actual chickpeas and provide them to the men with the flour mill to grind for them. However, even then, there was no way to know if other substances had been mixed into the flour to save costs.

'We would deliver 100–200 kilos of chickpeas to the flour mill and receive ground flour from them. The ritual was that my father would drop the chickpeas off and ask them, *"Bhai maal kaisa hai?"* The mill guys would respond with, "It is of excellent quality!" My father would take their word for it and carry on with his day,' said Manoharlal, exasperation peppering his voice.

After months of enduring the practice, Manoharlal finally insisted that the family change their ways. He wanted to control the inflow of raw materials to maintain quality and consistency of the final product. He was thinking years ahead of his fellow businessmen in Bikaner when considering the role of purchasing and its importance in laying down a strong supply chain. This was one of the key reasons behind Haldiram's success versus other packaged-food brands even up until the twenty-first century.

Manoharlal faced tremendous resistance at this suggestion. The family had built a relationship with the flour mill vendors, and breaking those bonds seemed almost like sacrilege to him. He also couldn't open his mind to the possibility that they might just be able to pull off grinding their own flour over and above other production responsibilities. Moolchand allegedly fumed about spoiled relationships with neighbours and inciting 'unnecessary quarrels' due to noise levels. He insisted that noise levels would disturb the peace of the neighbourhood. His son promised him that if a neighbour faced a problem, they would try to work with them to solve it. 'I told my father that if the neighbour had a problem with us installing a mill on our premises, then it's his problem! But if a neighbour is truly facing issues from the machine such as vibrations or sound, then we will work around it and ensure that it is used only during the time of the day agreed upon with the neighbour.' Manoharlal bided his time till his father's anger slightly dissipated before firmly informing him that they would cross that bridge when they came to it.

'Why restrict yourself based on what other people will say without even truly knowing if they will object or not?' Manoharlal said, truly perplexed. His practicality and disregard for the societal chains that had restricted the generation before his own had set him apart from the rest of the crowd. Even millennials in India have found breaking out of these traditional societal structures an extremely difficult task, and Manoharlal began his journey down this path at least a whole generation before the trend caught on.

Nonetheless, trouble with neighbours they did have. And it was big trouble in little Bikaner. The neighbour was furious, Moolchand was smug, but Manoharlal was stubborn as ever. In spite of the neighbour's anger and Moolchand's opposition, Manoharlal installed an industrial pulverizer in their tiny workshop. A friend of his had suggested that the pulverizer was a more convenient machine and was safer to use. Most importantly, it would make less noise than an actual flour mill. The grinding began and the Agarwals finally could use high-quality, pure besan without a shred of doubt from their own workshop. It also reduced the overall cost of besan from when they bought it from the flour mills. While the business benefited from this change, the neighbour was not pleased. The infuriated neighbour would regularly march over to their place, and a shouting match between the father, the son and the neighbour would ensue. Moolchand demanded that the pulverizer be removed, giving his neighbour full support in the fight. 'The neighbour's complaints were ridiculous!' said Manoharlal. 'He would say that all the utensils in his cupboards clanged when the pulverizer came on. How could that be possible when the utensils in our cupboard in the very same room did not make any noise? To top it all, their house was 50 feet away from ours!'

Manoharlal stood his ground, and to his father's embarrassment, locked horns with the neighbour every chance he could get. After weeks of this, eventually they came to an agreement. It was decided that Manoharlal would get rid of the pulverizer on the condition that he could, in its stead, install a flour mill. 'Oh, the irony!' He chuckles at the memory of his sweet victory to this day.

'I had conflicts with my father every step of the way,' confessed Manoharlal with a rueful smile. Father and son could never see eye-to-eye. Where Manoharlal was a hot-blooded passionate young man, his father was equally obstinate and steadfast in his beliefs. A man with old-school values, Moolchand came from an era where sons obeyed their fathers no matter what. Always obedient to Haldiram's wishes, Moolchand himself had begun religiously following some of his father's practices. He had become staunchly averse to taking loans to grow the business believing that a debt-free life translated to a stress-free one. While his beliefs had some merit, they at times stunted the growth of the business, restricting his sons from reaching their true potential. However, to be fair to him, he was a highly content man with no ambition or desire to grow, unable to understand and sympathize with his sons' hunger for success. In his reasoning, if one had enough food to feed the entire family, one could be truly content. To Manoharlal's extreme frustration, in such a scenario, Moolchand would ask, 'Why bother to take on more responsibilities or tension, and upset the gentle waves in the ocean of life?' However, while Manoharlal seemed to shrug these anecdotes off with a smile, in another conversation, Shiv Kishan could barely manage to disguise the disdain he felt at his father's 'lack of ambition'.

According to Manoharlal, Haldiram had the final say in everything. Together, the grandfather and father would resist every new idea put forth by the young Manoharlal, pushing him to inevitable acts of rebellion. Gradually, Manoharlal adopted and fiercely put into practice the philosophy of 'ask for forgiveness, not permission'.

It was only natural for the young hatchling to vigorously shake his feathers, struggle against the imposed restrictions and eagerly reach for the prize—the dangling juicy worm called progress. Let's stop to imagine Manoharlal's struggle in the '70s. The shop at Bikaner was producing 500–600 kilos of bhujia every month, which was a meagre amount compared to production in Kolkata. The margins were very low and the meagre profits were being shared by five stakeholders: Haldiram, Moolchand, Moolchand's second son, Shiv Ratan Agarwal, Manoharlal himself and the youngest brother, Madhusudan. The pie itself was so tiny that their individual pieces would probably have amounted to almost nothing. Manoharlal's constant struggle was focused on growing the size of that pie, making it bigger so there would be more for every stakeholder, and thereby more for the whole tribe.

Within a few years of Manoharlal joining the family business, Haldiram stopped visiting the factory. He continued the duty of being the first one in the morning to open the shop, but retired for the day by mid-morning. Moolchand, on the other hand, had never shown any inclination towards back-of-the-house activities. That left all day-to-day operational activities in Shiv Ratan and Manoharlal's purview. In spite of taking a back seat, Haldiram needed to be involved in every decision, big or small, when it came to his shop. The older generation's inability to give up control reveals a deeper desire to preserve their socio-emotional wealth. Growth entailed risk, and Haldiram was too anxious to even contemplate implementing a positive change if that meant the slightest possibility of losing his beloved business. That said, he had met his match in his clever, determined grandson.

Aside from steps taken to directly expand the business, the second major endeavour that Haldiram and Moolchand were staunchly against right from the get-go was packaging. Packaging eventually proved to be a game changer for the Haldiram family. Prabhu Shankar Agarwal, Rameshwarlal's son and current owner of the Kolkata business, said, 'Let it go on record that I said that packaging was the main reason behind all of our successes.' When proposed as packaging, it sounds rather simplistic. However, this one stroke of genius helped put the brand on the map through boosted awareness, helped it capture incremental market share through distribution, and gave them credibility globally of manufacturing high-quality products.

Manoharlal claims that since 1941, his grandfather had been doing business under the name Haldiram Bhujiawala. Haldiram had begun to use this name after he broke away from his grandfather's business in the same year. Allegedly, it was he who inaugurated the business in Kolkata around 1957–58 under the same name. These minute details will help unravel the labyrinth that is the brand battle between the Kolkata and Delhi units in the following chapters. The name 'Haldiram Bhujiawala' is important to the packaging story because up until the hot-headed Manoharlal decided to change the way things were done, nobody outside of Bikaner truly knew that they had bought their delicious bhujia from the 'Haldiram Bhujiawala' shop in Bikaner!

In 1963–64, packaging had evolved from bhujia being served in a rolled-up newspaper cone to bhujia being packed in a low-quality plastic bag. Bhujia would be poured in through the open end and the packet would be sealed with a few staples. The plastic bag was first 'branded', using letterpress, with the Haldiram Bhujiawala brand name. In the '40s and the '50s, only bhujia packed in tin containers meant for sale outside Bikaner and the display boards on the shops located in Bikaner contained the branding of Haldiram Bhujiawala. This ancient form of printing that had been in practice since the mid fifteenth century was still being used by most of India for multiple purposes. Letterpress had been designed to work on paper where the single ink would be absorbed by the surface. It entailed making a direct impression of a typeset on a raised surface on to the designated sheet. In the case of plastic, once a bag had been printed, a gentle brush of the fingers could make the ink smudge, and the multiple letters that made up the whole in 'Haldiram Bhujiawala' would magically disappear into a black swipe of untidiness.

'What was the point of such packaging?' Manoharlal asked no one in particular, still flabbergasted at the fact that they had ever used it. 'Most of our bhujia was purchased by merchants and travellers from areas outside Bikaner, such as Kolkata. We produced approximately 600 kilos of bhujia per month at the time and about 550 kilos out of the whole were sold to these merchants! Locally, every soul knew that the bhujia was from Haldiram Bhujiawala; however, with packaging—where the print was easily smudged with the touch of the hand—how would these merchants remember where and from whom they had bought the delicious namkeen?'

Bikaner, in those days, would see a barrage of Marwari traders from all over Rajasthan, Assam and West Bengal. These traders would come to visit family, conduct business and be off on their way once their purpose was fulfilled. Traders who knew the family well and truly appreciated the bhujia, sent letters in advance, informing the Haldiram Bhujiawala clan of their arrival, and placing orders for the bhujia. 'We used to be paid by demand draft for such orders,' said Manoharlal. 'Several of the other smaller shops also had some patrons who would place orders in advance, and if multiple bhujia brands were getting exported, then with the letterpress printing, ours could get lost in the crowd. We needed to have a recognizable brand. Of that, I was sure.'

Moreover, this packaging practice was extremely rudimentary and unhygienic. Workers would fill these plastic bags of bhujia by hand. With each bag filled, the branded ink would smudge further. The practice was a joke; the worker's hands grew dirtier as the print faded and this was then transferred on to the bhujia, as the process was manual. Bhujia with ink seemed to be the speciality of the times!

Disturbed, young Manoharlal broached the subject gently with his father. He questioned the practice and tried to deliver an impactful sales pitch demonstrating the wonderful effect a recognizable brand would have on their business. Demand would grow, they could eliminate competition and, most importantly, their product would instantly stand out not only because of branding, but because the absence of inky smudges would make the bhujia shine pure among the rest.

Moolchand, true to his reputation, was immediately defensive and against the change. His response according to Manoharlal was: 'Everyone is doing it. So obviously it is acceptable. Why should we change the packaging and increase our costs?' An indignant and frustrated Manoharlal argued with his father throwing emotional spears at him along the lines of 'Don't you want the business to grow? Don't you want to be recognized for your work?' Thus began another era of conflict between Manoharlal and his father.

By this time, though father and son loved each other dearly, there were several defensive walls between them, and regular conversation had become difficult. Neither was willing to accept, or even begin to understand, the other's point of view. Moolchand had written his son off as brazen and reckless. Manoharlal, on the other hand, believed that his father was far too conservative to even warrant further discussion and persuasion. The hunger was building in Manoharlal, and being a man of action, he needed to test his ideas. Unfortunately, when it came to Moolchand, ambition was not rewarded, and Manoharlal had to resort to subterfuge and secrecy in order to make his dreams come true.

'I was not one to be silenced easily,' he said, with a twinkle in his eye. It was right out of the movies. Manoharlal began meeting printing artists and having conversations with other forward-looking businessmen on better ways to package without his father's knowledge. He even made secret trips to Delhi in order to find the answer. Without the Internet, everything was done through word of mouth, and finding someone who knew someone who could perhaps introduce him to someone at a 'new and savvy' printing company took time and diligence. Finally, Manoharlal met some folks at Alphaflex Printing in Delhi who offered 'flexo printing' in multiple colours. Flexo printing was a modern form of letterpress but modified for all surfaces including plastic. For the late 1970s, these results were fabulous; multiple inks could be used and most importantly, the ink never smudged. Manoharlal requested a typeset for the famous V-shaped Haldiram Bhujiawala logo in two colours—white and red. There was a sense of adventure and thrill in getting everything set up in time to surprise his father. He also probably wanted to get it all done without any bickering during the process. While the printing was sophisticated and beautiful, there was definitely a catch—the cost was much higher than letterpress. With flexo printing, Manoharlal needed to make payments per piece, whereas with letterpress they paid per kilo. 'It was exorbitant for those days. Locally, we used to pay 10 paise per kilo of packets, but now we would need to shell out 15–16 paise per packet!' said Manoharlal.

He knew he would face a major pushback from his father and grandfather. He also realized that he had to make this decision carefully since it would affect everybody's lives. After all, they weren't the Birlas. Following much thought and some old-fashioned napkin calculations, Manoharlal decided it would be good for the business in the long run even though there might be some upfront costs to deal with. Armed with the freshly printed packets, Manoharlal tentatively introduced his grandfather and father to the modern concept of branding via packaging.

To nobody's surprise, fireworks followed. Not far behind them were typical Indian emotional tear-jerkers, meant to wear the opponent down. With his flair for drama, Moolchand asked his son, 'What will happen to our margins? What will we eat? How will we live?' However, Manoharlal had by then grown a thick skin and was able to withstand most of the storm. Moolchand wasn't way off the mark when he questioned the impact of flexo printing on the margins. At the time, the family made profits of 10–20 paise per kilo. Bhujia, as previously mentioned, was sold for ₹4–5 per kilo, clearly validating that the margins they earned were very low. According to Moolchand, if additional money now went into packaging, the family would be left with only a pittance.

All Manoharlal had was faith and a conviction in his belief that the flexo printing and more hygienic bhujia would increase demand, in turn giving them the opportunity to raise prices and snowballing their revenues into a different league. A sentiment that will resonate with most modern marketers—no amount of projections and speculations of growth guarantee success, only action could lead to such a desirable consequence.

'I asked him to give me time to try it and see if it would work out. My reasoning was: what's the worst that could happen? I promised that if in a few months the business did not take off like I predicted it would, then we would resort to the old way of packaging our products,' said Manoharlal. He strongly believed that every new initiative should be tried with enough time given to it for its potential to emerge.

Luckily, the business did take off. Traders specifically began asking for the Haldiram Bhujiawala product. The brand stood out amongst the crowd, and patrons of the smaller shops began switching over to Haldiram Bhujiawala. Demand increased to such an extent that the Haldiram Bhujiawala store began to have an increasing number of pending orders. The orders completely outnumbered their production capacity, which, of course, brought the family great joy and some riches, but also presented a new problem: capacity. Undoubtedly, as Manoharlal mentioned, it was better to have problems of surplus, than scarcity.

The Haldiram family, throughout its history, has unearthed a genius or rebel from each generation who insists on taking the road less travelled, pushing the family's thinking, forcing them to innovate and enabling them to reach newer heights of success. In the latter part of the twentieth century, Manoharlal proved to be that driving force, refusing to be tied down by the norm, eagerly grabbing every opportunity that presented itself. What set him apart was that, unlike his grandfather and his eldest brother, Shiv Kishan, Manoharlal made no attempt to blend his individualistic passions with their traditional culture. He broke free with his wings spread wide and courageously forged his own path against the hesitation of his family. This gave the business an edge it had never had before. Here was a young entrepreneur who pushed the boundaries and fearlessly tried uncharted waters to propel the business without fear of loss or failure. What set him apart was that he considered the safety of inaction and patience to be cumbersome vices.

It is a few men with bold attitudes who have always shaped the history of companies, cities and nations. The Haldiram family seemed to have always produced one such ambitious seeker in their midst in every generation, helping them climb the ladder of success.

## Fast and Furious

In the couple of years that he had worked in the family business, from 1975–77, Manoharlal had already made acutely impactful changes. The new packaging had set the brand apart, and everyone locally, as well as merchants from afar, had come to recognize the unique flavours of Haldiram's bhujia and begun associating it with the brand name. Manoharlal had also improved the quality of the actual product by carefully managing their purchasing process and installing gatekeepers to ensure that raw materials went through an exhaustive quality check before being used.

Even while demand surged, Manoharlal was convinced that they could sell much more. He felt that there was a huge market of merchants that they were not yet reaching because of their location. The current shop was in the heart of the bazaar and most travellers were not inclined to travel all that way just to purchase snacks on their way into or out of Bikaner. Scouting the Bhujia Bazaar area closer to the railway station, Manoharlal found several smaller bhujia shops making a profit based on purchases from travellers. Manoharlal knew it would be a huge missed opportunity to not move closer to the station. Now, a branded product that distinctly stood out from its competitors, Manoharlal felt that moving nearer to the station would definitely bring Haldiram Bhujiawala increased sales with greater impetus than ever before.

Eager to harness the reins of this new-found opportunity, Manoharlal reached out to a few friends, spreading the word silently through his network that he was looking for a shop in the Kolgate area near the station. Having learnt his lessons well, this time, Manoharlal discussed his plans with nobody from the family. Instead, he stealthily plotted, organized and implemented right under his father's nose.

In 1977, a few weeks after he put out word, a close friend came bearing good news. Motilal, a local businessman, and Manoharlal had started out as professional associates with deep respect for one another and had very quickly turned into close friends. Motilal had just heard of a shop becoming vacant in the Kolgate area. Knowing how popular the area was, he took Manoharlal to meet the landlord on the same day that he came to know about it. After inspecting the space and talking to the landlord, Manoharlal felt convinced that it was the perfect location. With the seller having more power in this situation, Manoharlal was pressurized into agreeing to purchase immediately or risk missing out on the opportunity. He chose the first option. The cost was ₹25,000, but the catch was that he had only two months to come up with the entire sum before the current owner vacated. Unable to organize a lump sum at that time, Motilal agreed to pay the advance for the shop with the promise that Manoharlal would pay him back in a couple of months. Knowing that Moolchand and Haldiram would be furious, Motilal was fully appreciative of his friend's situation and was completely at ease with waiting a couple of months to get his money back.

Once the advance was paid, Manoharlal got home and quietly went about his daily chores as if nothing had changed. The weeks following the surreptitious purchase became a highly nerve-racking waiting game for Manoharlal. He knew he would face the firing squad when he told them, but he still kept putting off the task of letting his father and grandfather know. He claims that he was exceptionally sensitive during those weeks, which in turn was borne out of intense guilt. His skin would crawl and he would jump at the slightest of questions and queries.

Two months seemed to pass very quickly and it was time to spill the beans. Manoharlal had had weeks to work on his courage and formalize a strategy to get his father and grandfather on board. He demonstrated patience, diplomacy and an incredible knack for smoothly manipulating his elders.

He went up to Moolchand and enthusiastically pitched the idea of moving closer to the railway station in Kolgate, elucidating the various benefits of the move. Once his father seemed to be theoretically in agreement with the idea, Manoharlal gently broke the news to him that he had booked a shop in the area. Moolchand was shocked and enraged that his son had not even consulted him before jumping into such a decision.

'I then told him that I had already paid the advance,' Manoharlal reminisced. 'His immediate response was, "Where did you get the money for it?" When I confirmed his worst fears that I had borrowed the money from a close friend, all hell broke loose!'

His father raved and ranted, pacing up and down on the ground floor of their house, his tirade subsiding after a little while. While Moolchand was mad, Manoharlal knew that his grandfather would be in a completely different league of anger. The difficulty for Manoharlal was that he knew his father could not help but share everything with Haldiram. He would tattle on about Manoharlal the first chance he got. In Manoharlal's own words, his father was a 'Shravankumar'. In the Ramayana, Shravankumar is depicted as a boy deeply devoted to his parents, i.e. the ever-obedient son. The legend goes, in their old age, his parents desirous of visiting the forty places of pilgrimage, requested their son to take them on this arduous journey. Faced with the unavailability of transport, Shravankumar tied two baskets at the ends of a long pole, one for each parent, and walked with the pole balanced on his back—thus enabling his elderly parents to complete their pilgrimage. Manoharlal believed Moolchand had the same blind obedience when it came to his father, Haldiram.

'My grandfather had a *gediya*—this wooden walking stick with a hook-like curve for a handle. He kept it with him at all times. It had multiple uses—at times he used it for support and at others to teach us a lesson!' said Manoharlal, grinning at the memory. 'So, at six the next morning, when I woke up and came downstairs, my father, grandfather and the beloved gediya lay in wait for me. This happened fairly regularly—my father would snitch to Haldiramji, using him as a weapon to set me straight.'

As most vicious cycles, this one had taken a habit-forming pattern. While it might sound unbelievable, Manoharlal would be spanked and shouted at, and after a lot of negotiations, finally be forgiven. By that time, he wasn't afraid of a few beatings. In fact, the young Manoharlal felt he wasn't doing something innovative or groundbreaking enough if he didn't get spanked for it.

So on that particular morning, a mentally prepared Manoharlal patiently received a walloping and a heavy stream of expletives thrown at him. Finally, in the lull before the storm, he asked them, 'Okay . . . so, now, are you going to give me the money?'

The gall the young man had! Haldiram apparently immediately responded, 'We will not buy the shop. I don't want it.' A sly Manoharlal put up a great show of meekly surrendering,

Haldiram—the only picture of him in the form
of a portrait hanging in Shiv Kishan's Nagpur office.

Champa Devi—Haldiram's wife.

Moolchand Agarwal—Haldiram's eldest son. This portrait too hangs in Shiv Kishan's Nagpur office.

Shiv Kishan Agarwal—Moolchand's eldes son, in all his Marwari glory.

Shiv Kishan and his wife during their early days in Nagpur.

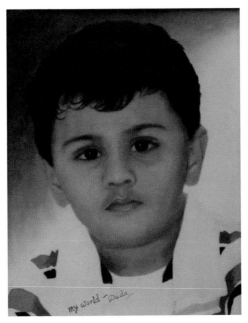

During his time in jail, Prabhu Agarwal painted this
portrait of his eight-year-old grandson.

Shiv Ratan Agarwal (sitting) and his son, Deepak Agarwal,
at the Bikaji office in Bikaner.

Worker piling heaps of bhujia at the Bikaji factory, Bikaner.

Hygiene and safety matter at the state-of-the-art
air-conditioned bhujia-making facility at Bikaji.

The first Delhi showroom has grown in size since it was set up in 1983.

Ashish Agarwal, one of the youngest heirs to Haldiram's Delhi, at his Noida office.

The Haldiram's showroom in Gurgaon.

Diwali sweets and gift boxes in the Delhi showroom.

Automated factories under Manoharlal's forward-looking reign.

The prodigy: Pankaj Agarwal.

Moolchand's sons: (L–R) Madhusudan Agarwal, Shiv Kishan Agarwal (sitting), Shiv Ratan Agarwal and Manoharlal Agarwal.

'Okay, I'll refuse to take it in that case . . . I'll let them know that we no longer want it and ask them to return our advance.'

Haldiram thundered with exasperation, 'How can we refuse now? We have given our word! What will people think? That Haldiram goes back on his word? This will reflect badly on me!'

'I knew that while Haldiramji was principled against ever taking a loan to grow the business, he was even more staunch about keeping his word. My plan had worked! Haldiramji would never allow his reputation to become tarnished and he was extremely proud to be known as a man who kept his word,' said Manoharlal with a sense of accomplishment.

Manoharlal had used Haldiram's principles against him, knowing fully well which one of them Haldiram would adhere to more strongly. He had known that Haldiram would never go back on his word whether it had been given by him or spoken on his behalf. However, Manoharlal's intentions had been pure— he was driven to grow the business and make it successful. He knew that if he didn't push the boundaries, nobody else would. 'If I had ever only worked following all their rules, I would have made no progress.'

Haldiram was incredibly unhappy about the situation. However, having been pushed into a corner, he had had to allow his grandson to pay the amount for the new shop. He did this all the while berating Manoharlal for not taking his feelings into consideration.

The following day, Haldiram, Moolchand, Shiv Ratan and Manoharlal were proud owners of a second shop in the Kolgate area. Being locals, they could quickly send hands from the old shop in Bachaut Ka Mohalla to the one in Kolgate to set up the business. They were selling at maximum capacity almost from day one, with an increasing number of travellers making purchases before catching the train. Soon, relatives and friends of traders began requesting their products, and their fame grew. The order amounts also began increasing in spite of the low shelf life of about one week. People were taking five to ten kilos of bhujia in one go. It was a glorious period of growth with soaring sales and turnover.

Once their bhujia had become well known to customers outside Bikaner, they started producing a few additional items. The initial product line expansion was very simple, with them adding a couple more of different types of bhujia to the line. In addition to their famous skinny, spicy bhujia, they began selling moti bhujia, which they called 'No. 3 Bhujia', and hard bhujia to make dry stir-fry vegetables called 'Sabziwali Bhujia'. Seeing the success of these, they also introduced a few varieties of mixtures, which were received with a moderate level of demand. Within a year, production went up to 1200 kilos a month for all three types of bhujia together.

Location-based strategies are often not given their due. Being in the Kolgate area made them even more prevalent as the brand gained prominence among both locals as well as outsiders. Brand recognition combined with increasing sales positively impacted the goodwill value of the brand, and the family began to take great pride in their handiwork. With fame came even more possessiveness and commitment to the business. With success came an intense desire to keep growing and maintain that status.

In 1978, the relationship between father and son took a turn for the better. With the fruits of Manoharlal's labour in front of his eyes, Moolchand could no longer deny his son some autonomy. 'After setting up the shop in Kolgate, my father began to have confidence in me. He stopped giving me a hard time and realized that I had not only bettered the product and its quality, but I had also doubled and tripled our sales.' Manoharlal finally had his father's respect, but not his unwavering support, which he realized only when the time came to move to Delhi.

However, in the meantime, Moolchand was pleased with the results of changing the packaging, improving the product and adding another shop location. He was convinced that Manoharlal had been blessed with a shrewd mind and keen business acumen. A year following the second shop, they were considered a higher quality product compared to those available in the market and could raise prices by 10–20 paise per kilo. Being a branded product definitely had its advantages.

In spite of this upward spiral, the family also faced some very difficult times. A lot seemed to happen in a few short years. In 1978, Moolchand developed a heart disease and took a backseat in the business, entrusting his sons with all day-to-day responsibilities. And then, in 1980, Haldiram shockingly passed away. It was a heartbreaking day for the family, for they had come to deeply rely on the great patriarch for advice, support and guidance. What made it even more difficult to accept was that he was healthy up until his dying day, making his passing away extremely unexpected. However, it is said that he died a content man. While Moolchand had never inspired his sons to greatness, Haldiram had borne that mantle throughout his life, and had left his grandsons with a deep desire to make and sell the best quality bhujia. They, of course, took the legacy to new heights.

By 1981–82, the production had gone up to 3000 kilos per month, a whopping 400 per cent increase in just five years. 'I remember when I created the P&L statement for 1982 and showed it to my father, he was so astonished by our profit margins,' said Manoharlal. 'His awed response was, "Could there be so much profit? I never dreamed we could make so much."' Seeing those sheets, in that moment, Manoharlal confessed that his father finally began to feel confident in the strength of the business.

In spite of the fact that Moolchand had never been a 'great businessman' role model for Manoharlal, all his memories indicated that winning his father's approval had meant a lot to him. In all his rebellions, what he longed for most were his father's trust and faith in his abilities and his vision. Having earned his father's confidence, and experienced success himself as a result of his hard work, Manoharlal was ready to jump into the playing field amid the big guns to take on the capital.

## Capital Gains

In the search for ways to fulfil basic human needs over the millennia, mankind has evolved from being early hunters and gatherers to sophisticated bankers, engineers and doctors. As more of the lowest-level needs were fulfilled, man's basic requirements rose up Maslow's pyramid to include intangibles like self-esteem and pride. In the distant past, security had meant shelter against rain and storm, harsh rays of the sun and the bitter cold. It had meant food to survive and a way to keep one's family safe. With inventions born out of necessities, man evolved from living in a barter society to thriving in modern civilization where paper notes became the form of currency. Above all, man's survival instinct urged him to protect his own by fortifying his home and his assets.

Well out of poverty, running successful business units that provided the family with 'a roof over their heads, warm beds to sleep at night and food to fill their stomachs' as Moolchand would say, was not enough for Haldiram's grandchildren. They wanted more. More power, more security, more success. Once they knew it could be had, the slight discomfort of growing desires gave them the necessary impetus to throw caution to the wind and follow their hearts on the path to greater triumph. United by the common vision of conquering Delhi, Manoharlal and Shiv Kishan worked together to achieve this goal.

While Manoharlal had been busy bringing the Bikaner business up to standard, his eldest brother, Shiv Kishan had been undergoing his own journey to make something of himself in Nagpur. Having established a successful business in Nagpur, Shiv Kishan was hungry to tap into his own potential and take the Haldiram Bhujiawala brand to greater heights. The brothers began dreaming and building castles in the air as early as 1975. Multiple phone conversations later, Manoharlal and Shiv Kishan met in Delhi to put their money where their mouths were.

In 1976 they took their first step in what they considered a lower risk area, Fatehpur, a small town on the outskirts of Delhi. Through word of mouth, the brothers learnt that a shop owned by J.B. Mangharam, a famous manufacturer of sweets from Gwalior, was becoming vacant. Buying the shop seemed like a great deal at the time, and the fact that the shop was already set up with the right countertops and arrangement to serve as a food-store was very exciting for them. As all things that come easily, this find was too good to be true. Manoharlal gave the owner of that shop ₹30,000 as an advance for booking it and he never saw the shop or his advance ever again. The brothers had been swindled out of their money!

'We tried moving to Delhi a couple of times and lost our advance money both those times!' said Manoharlal, amused at their past naivety. While ₹30,000 seems a petty amount to the business magnate today, it was a considerable sum for them in those days. However, the brothers couldn't give up. They kept their attempts to move to Delhi hidden from their father, and secretly continued to dream and plot their grand entrance into the capital.

In 1982, the brothers came across a shop that struck a chord deep within. It was a tiny space of about eight-by-eleven feet and yet, its location in Chandni Chowk made it perfect for them. The deposit for the shop was a reasonable amount at ₹2100, but the cost of ownership was ₹10 lakh, a significant amount. The brothers, however, felt they could somehow pull it off. With the advance paid, they were now faced with the larger conundrum of winning their father over.

They didn't tell their father. It was agreed that if push came to shove, they could in the short term sacrifice their move to Delhi, in case Moolchand was heartbroken beyond reproach. After all, the advance was a reasonably small sum of money that they both agreed would be worth taking the hit for, since the shop was one that met their dream standards. 'We hoped that accepting the fact that we had paid an advance for a shop in Delhi would not be as big a deal for father as the one in Kolgate had been. In Bikaner, it had been a matter of pride and integrity and maintaining our reputation by not going back on our word; however, in Delhi, we were an unknown entity, which made the matter of our reputation a moot point. The exit strategy seemed less painful than the time when I had bought the shop in Kolgate.' said Manoharlal. They hoped that if the exit strategy were less risky, then Moolchand would be more amenable to investing in the shop in Delhi.

The brothers cooked up an elaborate plan to introduce Moolchand to their ambitions. It's amazing what the fear of parents can do for kids' creativity. That same year, in the month of May, Shiv Kishan's eldest son, Rajendra Agarwal, was getting married. The whole clan from Bikaner travelled to Nagpur for the wedding festivities. It was planned that on the way back, Shiv Kishan would escort his father and Manoharlal to the halfway home, to Delhi, under the pretext of spending more time with them. While Moolchand didn't have any inkling as to what the sons had done, he was definitely suspicious that something was up. Unfortunately for them, neither of the brothers exhibited great talent for subtlety.

Once in Delhi, they quickly checked into their hotel room and asked their father if he would be interested in checking out the famous Chandni Chowk market. Moolchand was immediately on guard, his sixth sense as a parent giving out a silent alarm that the kids were up to no good. Apparently, he innocently queried, 'Why? What work do I have in the market?'

The conversation unravelled something like this.

'Let's just check it out, Babuji.'

'But why?' Moolchand stood his ground.

'It might be interesting. So many snack shops around, we might learn something.'

'What do we have to learn from these Delhi shops? We're doing fine in Bikaner.'

After much back and forth, Manoharlal couldn't help himself and burst forward with his confession, 'I've given the advance for a shop . . .'

Silence followed. As their nervousness rose, Moolchand asked, 'How much is it for?'

'Ten lakh,' came the meek reply.

This time the brothers got what they had been expecting all along—an explosion.

'And where may I ask will this ten lakh come from?' cried Moolchand.

Manoharlal and Shiv Kishan immediately tried reassuring their father.

They told him that they planned to invest five lakhs each in the shop, and that way they could wing it.

'I know you'll wing it, but I want to know how much you have,' replied Moolchand sternly.

Shiv Kishan answered first, 'I currently have four lakhs, and the rest I will be able to manage by the time we have to pay up.'

Moolchand then looked questioningly at Manoharlal, who said, 'I have three and a half to four lakhs. The rest of the shortfall I will also manage.'

Moolchand continued his relentless questioning. 'Yes, yes. I know you can manage anything. But I want to know exactly how you will *wing* it.' He continued making some very valid points around the reality that the ₹10 lakh would not be where the expenditure would stop. In order to set up, buy furniture, get production going, the brothers would need at least ₹15–16 lakh at a minimum.

'Have you even thought this through?' he asked his sons, his voice tinged with sarcasm.

Manoharlal jumped up to defend their plan, saying, 'Let us at least purchase the shop space now. It's an amazing opportunity given its location. We will take six months to a year to save enough money to get production going. The property will give impetus to our plans.'

Moolchand, however, was not impressed. He insisted on seeing a breakdown of their liquid assets before considering what he called a 'rash plan'. Manoharlal smiled as he recounted the episode: 'I gave him a breakdown of every last rupee. However, even with a reasonable amount of exaggeration, I could not come up with anything more than four lakhs. I described how we would take ₹50,000 from this account and some more money from another account. It was ridiculous how tight we were on that budget!'

Shiv Kishan was in a better position. His four lakhs were concrete on paper and he assured Moolchand that he would manage the remaining one lakh.

'Yes, but how exactly will you *manage?*' thundered the exasperated father.

'At this point we were at our wits' end!' said Manoharlal laughing. 'I blurted out that if we couldn't make the stretch and find that final one or one and a half lakhs, we could ask our uncle Rameshwarlal in Kolkata for help. My reasoning was that he was doing better than any of us at the time. All of West Bengal had gone to him, after all. But herein lay my folly.'

Moolchand suddenly shut down and would not hear another word that sounded remotely like a loan from anywhere. He immediately declared that nobody would buy a shop in Delhi. Panicking, the brothers realized that they had inadvertently hit a raw nerve. Not only was Moolchand highly principled about not taking loans, he found the very idea of borrowing from his brother exceedingly unpalatable.

Backtracking, Manoharlal and Shiv Kishan reassured their father that they would not borrow from anyone; they would earn the money themselves. They asked him for his trust and promised to stand on their own two feet if and when they entered Delhi.

Hours of conversation would have no meaning if Moolchand did not share their vision. They persuaded him to at least take a look at the shop, and incredibly, that did the magic. Seeing the shop on a *manch* (pedestal, higher ground) at Fountain, in the very heart of the market, Moolchand himself could not deny that it was very well situated for their purpose. His heart melted and he finally relented, and agreed with his sons that if they met his condition of not taking on any debts, they were free to purchase the shop in Chandni Chowk. And thus began the Delhi chapter of the saga.

There was simplicity and a very small-town mentality to their initial foray into Delhi. Their goals were directly proportional to their means, while their dreams sparkled like the store lights glittering in Connaught Place. They had high hopes, and the setbacks only meant that they needed to work harder to achieve them. But obstacles lay waiting ahead, ready to dampen their heady idealism with a dark deposit of cynicism, starting with the Sikh riots in 1984.

Nonetheless, the days of setting up in Delhi were filled with a sense of indefatigable faith. 'The day we made the payment for the shop, that very day we pushed the dealer to look for a workshop for us. Now that the Delhi adventure was beginning, our impatience was mounting,' said Manoharlal, lost in the glory of the past. 'After much haranguing, he told us that the only place that we could get within our budget was a roof above a baker's shop. He convinced us that our only chance of getting a workshop space was to build over that roof. So I said, okay ... give us the roof!'

They gave the dealer a small advance with the agreement that they would cough up the rest of the amount within three months.

'Sales in Nagpur were always incredibly high during Diwali. In spite of the restrictions placed by Father, I could save ₹2 lakh that went towards the roof. Manoharlal worked towards arranging the remaining ₹1.5 lakh. It was a great victory, a rush of pride at making the dream come true in spite of Father's scepticism,' said Shiv Kishan. Following the grand purchase, Shiv Kishan returned to Nagpur to continue looking after the business there, while Manoharlal began working towards practically making the move happen.

Once the roof was paid for, Manoharlal travelled to Delhi to ensure that three storeys were built above the roof, creating both living quarters as well as a workshop. All of which went up in smoke a year later during the 1984 riots.

By 1985, once the second workshop had been built and the floors above the baker's shop had been repaired, Manoharlal had become a workaholic in order to strengthen the business and make sure the family would never again be vulnerable in the face of any disasters or troubles. In 1986, the building behind theirs became vacant in the Katara Lachchu Singh area. Manoharlal and his younger brother, Madhusudan Agarwal, purchased the space. Production increased and, slowly and steadily, so did the number of workshops. Soon after, they purchased another construction in Ghantewali Gali, beginning production of snacks there as well. Manoharlal was expanding at a rate unseen by any of his predecessors. He worked with immense fervour, motivated by ensuring the security of his business. In spite of the incremental production, they never had to worry about a warehouse space as everything they produced was sold out almost immediately. The demand for their snacks and sweets was insane and spurred their growth at the time. Forced to keep pace, in the late '80s, Manoharlal bought a 2000-square-metre area in Mathura Road, the first of their steps to move out of Chandni Chowk, towards conquering all of Delhi. They built their factory on the plot and began wholesale distribution for the first time. Distribution put them on the map. They no longer needed customers to visit their shop to make purchases but could reach customers through a network of retailers and smaller shops. It did wonders for the brand awareness as well.

Haldiram's was already one of the most recognizable Indian brands in north India by the early 1990s. Multinationals such as P&G and PepsiCo began keeping an eye on them, nervous about their competitive presence in India. It was rumoured that PepsiCo offered to buy Haldiram's when they entered the Indian market after liberalization. Gurcharan Das, president of P&G and author of multiple books, mentions in his book *The Elephant Paradigm* that there were only two new brands in the market demonstrating world-class skill and performance—and Haldiram's was one of them. He went on to laud Haldiram's on putting up a 'solid fight' to maintain their business and hold on to their socio-emotional wealth.

Pramod Tapadia praised his dearest friend Manoharlal on his staunch self-belief and strength of character in not giving in to PepsiCo, to which Manoharlal immediately put up a show of humility and said it was all 'nothing'. After some gentle prodding, Manoharlal confirmed that PepsiCo had approached him to buy out Haldiram's. 'They wanted us to produce namkeens for them which they could brand as PepsiCo products. We might have entered into an agreement to help with their production had they not insisted that we give up selling under our own brand, that we stop Haldiram's! I refused to give up our brand, our dream.'

Looking back, these foreign companies had a great deal of resources and pull. Standing their ground as an upcoming family business without much monetary might was a brave step to take. 'The irony is that PepsiCo Lehar then started making traditional namkeens themselves and never quite came close to Haldiram's success in the space,' said the proud friend and ally, Pramod Tapadia.

They might have lacked the resources that these multinational players had at their disposal, but what they lacked in financial resources they made up in their knowledge of the local customers and, more importantly, their strong relationships with suppliers and karigars in the market. Tapadia said, 'Gurcharan Das had once mentioned that part of the reason why Haldiram's was successful was due to their strong relationships within the market—and he was right.'

A majority of the karigars who worked at Haldiram's had come to the city with them from Bikaner. As the business grew, so did its local workforce. In fact, many of the karigars who had helped open the first shop in Chandni Chowk have become loyal managers of the brand's various showrooms and restaurants across the north today. Manoharlal himself confessed that having a loyal workforce, dedicated to the brand and family, gave the business a solid infrastructure to stand upon. Manoharlal quietly said, 'Having a strong workforce is a God-given boon. For these workers to work with as much dedication and faith in the business as we have, was our good fortune.' At which point Tapadia jumped in: 'Manoharlal's best and worst quality is that he never accepts credit for his achievements but wants to constantly and generously distribute it.' That left Manoharlal muttering, 'How can I take credit for what is not in my hands?'

Realizing that they had an audience, Manoharlal couldn't help but exchange an uncomfortable grin with his friend. He sighed and, nodding to Tapadia, said, 'We have always treated them like family. My doors are always open to everybody—from the peon to the oldest karigars. I am willing to meet with them and learn from them. In fact, some of my senior management complains about how this disrupts the line of hierarchy where the workers tend to overreach and come see me instead of them. It takes away the necessity of our layers, they say. However, my argument to meeting them is always, "Why would any worker come and see me? He would only come if he felt that nobody else could solve his problems. And so I have an obligation to meet him."'

Manoharlal, in that instant, had unknowingly given an insight into the inner workings of the current business. The old family business had never had any layers between the owners and the workers. The relationship was direct and strong, part of why the workforce had always been so loyal to the family. They had been made to feel like friends, like comrades, like partners who had an equal stake in the growth of the business. However, today, as the business modernizes, it faces the challenge of maintaining those touch points in spite of the increasing degrees of separation. Through multiple conversations with the staff and his sons, this aspect of blending new employees with the old is an uphill challenge the company is currently facing, as we'll come to appreciate in later chapters through Pankaj Agarwal, Manoharlal's eldest son.

The early '90s were an era of great strength for the Delhi business. While the young scion had built a great foundation for his enterprise—quality, strength in relationships, and distribution networks, the '90s were also an era where Manoharlal and his brothers began facing their greatest trial— one from within the family. The Kolkata and Delhi units began their continuing twenty-four-year-old feud, becoming impediments to their own greatness. In 1991, the Delhi unit abandoned the traditional brand name of Haldiram Bhujiawala and rebranded to Haldiram's, as we know them today. While the public only saw a name change and continued to love the new brand as much as—or perhaps even more than—the previous one, the family itself underwent an ordeal of anger, betrayal and a clash of egos. Both sides bitterly point fingers at each other. Both sides righteously believe in their own cause, and the feud continues at the cost of millions of rupees and thousands of billable hours. Yet, determining which party's conscience is clearer is an impossible take—much like trying to separate the waters of two oceans.

# PART IV

# THE BLACK SHEEP

# Man behind the Myth

Notorious stories of bribes, blackmail and bullying abound in Hindi films and are often heard of in the form of gossip in business circles that most ordinary people are not privy to. One is always curious to read about businessmen, and the lengths they are willing to go to for their businesses. These leave us with a sense of amazement that they pulled it off, indignation that they managed to get away with it, and a mixture of disgust and admiration that they had the mettle to actually think of such deeds and implement them. Prabhu Shankar Agarwal was one such businessman. Over the years, Prabhu Shankar had received a lot of bad press for myriad reasons. Where the press was concerned, he had more than earned his disrepute. The journey to Kolkata to meet Prabhu Shankar, Rameshwarlal's eldest son was fraught with nerves and trepidation. In Kolkata, he was notorious for his boisterous ways and for allegedly being unafraid of bending the law to achieve his goals. The man seemed to have a lot of clout in the state and the thought of meeting him face-to-face and asking him not just questions, but difficult queries about his life and business, was daunting.

One is almost tempted to find parallels with Mario Puzo's Godfather clan. Men who believed in their mission and purpose and made no compromises in the methods they deployed in going after their goals. Imagine meeting Michael Corleone in person. It was only at the thought of an actual tête-à-tête that the true insecurity or terror of meeting a man as powerful as Prabhu Agarwal—with allegedly few to no scruples—sunk in. Prabhu Shankar Agarwal, the fifty-six-year-old owner of the famous Haldiram Bhujiawala business in Kolkata, has gained quite a reputation in business circles in Kolkata and nationally. On 5 June 2005 Prabhu was arrested for allegedly attempting to murder a teashop owner in order to gain access to his land, which was directly in front of a food mart that he was building. The charge sheet was filed a year later. In 2010 Prabhu was tried in a fast track court and was declared guilty and sentenced to life imprisonment by Judge Tapan Sen on 29 January 2010.[3] Spending several months in jail, however, did little to affect his business. Haldiram Bhujiawala, under the guidance of this dynamic leader, has continued to prosper.

Prabhu Agarwal was the proverbial elephant in the room during every conversation with the Haldiram family. In spite of being far from Bikaner and Delhi, he seemed to be present in spirit among them through words both spoken and unspoken. While newspaper articles had portrayed this businessman as a murderous convict lacking scruples, one naturally expected family members to defend and justify his actions. But it was not so. In fact, the members of the family in Delhi and Bikaner were distinctly uncomfortable about questions on Prabhu and made no move to defend his actions. With rumours abound,

---

[3] 'Haldiram Owner, 4 Others Get Life Imprisonment in Murder Case', *Times of India*, 29 January 2010. http://timesofindia.indiatimes.com/city/kolkata/Haldiram-owner-4-others-get-life-imprisonment-in-murder-case/articleshow/5513634.cms.

having heard multiple stories about him, it would be really easy to form preconceived opinions about the man. However, landing in Kolkata forced me to realize that up to that point, the man had been an enigma—a great businessman, shrewd and tough, capable of going to great lengths to grow his business, maybe even murder! One couldn't tell how he would measure up against all the varying descriptions about him.

Prabhu Shankar Agarwal inspired discomfort, fear and distaste among his family members, yet there was also an underlying awe for his persona and bold actions. While largely diplomatic, family members almost couldn't help themselves as they divulged their feelings about the owner of the Kolkata Haldiram Bhujiawala. Words such as 'greed', 'selfishness', 'unpredictable', 'temper', 'ambitious' and 'secretive' made their rounds in the descriptions. But as the conversations deepened and family members felt more and more comfortable, reluctant praises such as 'dynamic', 'keen business acumen', 'strong' and 'visionary' tumbled unwarranted into the parley. The man was a paradox, both notorious and private, all at once. It is said that nobody knows which version of him they would meet on any given day.

At 11 a.m. sharp, on the designated day, checking in with the receptionist on the second floor at the Kazi Nazrul Islam Avenue showroom, it was impossible not to feel nervous about meeting Prabhu Agarwal. This was Haldiram Bhujiawala's largest showroom in the city and also the headquarters of the company. Waiting in the reception area as the *malik*, or owner, finished his rounds of the ornate showroom floor below, one couldn't help but admire the beautiful painting covering the wall behind the receptionist's desk, depicting the opulent showroom building, glorious in the pink rays of the dawn, decorated by a single ornament, the 'Haldiram Bhujiawala' signboard. The outlet was definitely lavish compared to showrooms in any other city, including Delhi. There seemed to be something slightly classy about it, which was reflected in the painstaking way in which trays of sweets and snacks had been arranged in alcoves and on stations, brightened by flattering yellow lighting in the right places. The showroom was large with a huge room on the side, serving as the restaurant. Unlike the other Haldiram brand showrooms in Nagpur and Delhi, this one seemed to be catering to a more high-end crowd, with sophisticated tastes. However, Prabhu would vehemently disagree. 'Look at our reasonable prices,' he said in justification, claiming that the middle-class Indian was their primary target customer group. He strongly believed his target customers had sophisticated tastes.

While store design and in-store branding had hardly ever been an overarching strategy, nonetheless, they reflected Prabhu Agarwal's innate understanding of aesthetics and desire for great presentation. An entourage of men barged into the reception area. The short, portly man in the front of the group exuded a bustling energy that swept up everyone in its path. Prabhu Agarwal had a very cheerful air about him, with sparkling bright eyes and a keen friendly manner. Having shaken my hand and introduced himself with a beaming smile on his face, he apologized for making me wait and asked me to follow him into his office, while at the same time launching numerous commands at his staff. He seemed involved in all the intricate details of his business, discussing the design of a new workshop floor, arguing with an engineer about the dimensions of a required machine and working with his secretary to clear his schedule for the next few hours. Finally, he offered me his undivided attention.

Prabhu came across as an impatient perfectionist with both vitality and grace. He was a man of action and seemed to be able to multitask even while answering questions. Unlike his Delhi and Nagpur cousins, he seemed to also have a sharpened media awareness compelling him to put his best foot forward in front of outsiders. What piqued my curiosity was that in spite of his friendliness, he also seemed to exhibit a wariness of unknown entities. Sometime during our conversations he confessed that he had been watching me silently on the showroom floor before I made my way to the reception area. He had watched me admire the stands, talk to his employees and formed certain opinions about me, before he came to greet me with great aplomb. It subtly gave away the man's lack of trust in most people. However, it also indicated that Prabhu Agarwal was always primed for battle and never as unassuming as he made himself out to be.

Slightly wary, he answered almost every question posed to him with a counter-question. It seemed he had come prepared not to say anything politically incorrect. While most of the other Haldiram progenies had started conversations with a slightly humble, diplomatic opening such as, 'What can I tell you that others haven't already?' Prabhu Agarwal constantly asked, 'What did they tell you in Nagpur and Bikaner? I will be more comfortable to talk to you once I know what they said.'

Born in 1959 in Kolkata, Prabhu Agarwal had lived his whole life in the bustling postcolonial city. A few years younger than even his cousin Manoharlal, Prabhu had missed most of the early action in Kolkata. By the early 1970s, when Prabhu began helping around in the shop and learning about the business, he was already heir to the largest outfit of the Haldiram businesses since at that time the Kolkata branch made the highest margins and the greatest sales compared to Bikaner and Nagpur. Everything he had learnt about entrepreneurship and making bhujia, he had learnt from his father, Rameshwarlal. In spite of never having lived in Bikaner, unlike every other Agarwal man from his generation or previous ones, Prabhu had imbibed the same ingenious skill of identifying spices and mixing fabulous snacks from scratch.

In fact, when young, his love for the family business constantly stole him away from regular studies. He studied up to the higher secondary level at Shri Didu Maheshwari Panchayat Vidhyalaya in Bada Bazaar. While he found every excuse to skip classes and help out in the shop's kitchen, his father rarely rewarded him for his enthusiasm. 'I was given a lot of tough love for trying to join work that early. My father was not happy because unlike him, he wanted me to study further and gain a proper education.

'However, I was always the student who was first from the bottom!' said Prabhu with a guffaw. While largely uninterested in studies, Prabhu was deeply affected by the words of one Hindi professor whom the children called RD out of affection. 'RD always said, "The man who works never loses. The reward will find you some day, somehow." These words left a lasting impression on me and have ever since always proved true, at least in my life,' he said.

He began by working at the cash counters, helping with billing and accounting. His knack for numbers and understanding of the use of promotions such as discounts to make a profit quickly, shone through. In fact, even today, he readily admits that practical education behind a cash counter takes someone way farther than any structured educational programme can. When asked how long his training lasted, he said with a smile, 'It's going on even today.'

More seriously, he confessed that while he had learnt the ability to taste for ingredients, manage the business and remain strong in the face of major challenges from his father, Rameshwarlal, he had not acquired his acute desire for success from him. Rather, he believed that he had greater ambition than most men in his family and that men from his father's generation had not been truly forward looking. However, he couldn't help but be proud of his father's skill at namkeen-making.

It is claimed that Rameshwarlal was the best taster in his family, for his time. He could tell you what type of oil had been used in a dish including insane amounts of detail around those ingredients. For instance, if he had identified that peanut oil had been used, he could almost accurately guess what percentage of moisture the original peanuts had contained. 'They used to call him Laboratory,' said Mahesh Agarwal, Prabhu's younger brother and owner of Pratik Foods Ltd, with pride. Rameshwarlal had also learnt a great deal about the Bengali market and the tastes of the customers during his years in Kolkata. He was known for his calm, collected temperament, and both sons admit that they had never seen their father exhibit any signs of stress in spite of demanding conditions at work. 'Father always used to say, if a train is going from Delhi to Kolkata, given our population, no matter how many passengers get off at a particular station, three times their number would get on!' said Mahesh. Rameshwarlal had great faith in destiny. He believed that while in life there

would be multiple ups and downs, in the end everything would
even out.

Unlike his brother Moolchand, Rameshwarlal was industrious
and ambitious at least to the extent of wanting to run a profitable
and growing enterprise. He, however, according to his sons,
lacked strategic foresight or the desire to soar above the skies.
'Men of those times, they did not have dreams. They were so
busy keeping their head above the water and tending to their
daily responsibilities that they could never plan for the future.
For my father, growth happened through a one-plus-one-plus-
one organic forward movement or rather through serendipitous
moves,' said Prabhu. While his father had been plagued by daily
toils, Prabhu and his sons dreamt fearlessly of the future and
visualized the potential expanse of their empire. Mahesh seemed
to have a differing viewpoint from his brother. 'Father wanted
to grow the business but not so much that it would become an
uncontrollable obsession. He always advised us to work as much
as required to have a happy, comfortable life,' he said. While
both sons admired their father's calm ways, some of his peace-
loving actions might have had serious repercussions on their
lives in the form of the brand battle that began in the early '90s,
as we will see later.

Rameshwarlal believed that no problem was undefeatable,
demonstrating a great deal of poise and strength in the face
of challenges such as major union struggles and professional
setbacks. Instead of having an emotional reaction, he would
immediately set his mind to finding a solution to the problem,
a trait that was apparently not passed down to his eldest son,
Prabhu. However, he did set an example for his son on always
picking up the pieces and standing strong.

As kids, Prabhu and Mahesh would go to the showroom every day unless they were faced with highly extenuating circumstances. They were incentivized by money, of course! Rameshwarlal said that if they went to the shop and spent even half an hour there, they would earn 50 paise to a rupee. In this way, the boys earned their pocket money but also subconsciously began to understand the mechanisms of running a shop and the needs of the customers. 'We used to call it *galle ka paisa* since it came from the petty cash drawer. If we didn't go to the shop, we wouldn't receive the money. At that age, it was a very tempting proposition. Whether we helped out at the shop for five minutes or a whole hour, we always received the same amount. It was a very clever ploy. I suppose father hoped that our natural curiosity would be piqued with time, and boy was he lucky that it did!' said Mahesh. While Mahesh spoke about the pocket money, Prabhu's recollections give an insight into what makes him tick as a person. 'It was also a great thrill when the staff called us "malik" at that young age and treated us with immense respect, the same that was given to the big boss! It made us feel important. I think the whole experience also taught us the value of money—that it was in reality always tied to something,' he said. Perhaps it was then that he also realized a mesmerizing truth, that money was also directly linked to power.

However, while he was alive, Rameshwarlal never allowed his sons to abuse the power of their growing inheritance. Like his father and brothers before him, he had also imbibed the inherent sense of investing profits back into the business. Money earned from the business was not meant to be squandered away on other luxuries, but instead ploughed back to further nourish the business. All the Haldiram progeny seemed to be very proud of this trait, believing that it differentiated them from several other business families that never made it. A shared principle was that man should have control over money, not the other way around. However, while some brothers seemed to have been able to live by this oath, others have let burgeoning ambition get the better of them.

'I remember when I was really young, my father and I were walking down the street and I came across some raffle tickets where you could win something if you got the lucky number,' recalled Mahesh. 'I was very excited and unabashedly begged him to buy me one.' But he said, "You'll pull the ticket but you don't know what you'll receive. Instead, why don't you tell me exactly which toy you want from the lottery items box and I will buy it for you? That is a guarantee for getting what you want. Why gamble when you can be sure?" This stayed with me for a long time. Destiny is of our making and luck has nothing to do with it.'

Prabhu added a few more layers to their shared philosophy. 'When you simply win or receive ₹100, you only have a momentary thrill but it doesn't last. You always wonder—what if I had won ₹50 more? On the other hand, if you lose even one rupee, you feel miserable. That's because what you have, you have earned and it has great value.' While this ideology is not justification for some of his questionable actions, it definitely provides an understanding into the inner philosophies of a man who went on to allegedly attempt murder to expand and preserve his business.

# Tragedies and Triumphs

Even though Kolkata is India's second largest city in terms of population, it has never been considered truly cosmopolitan when compared to Delhi or Mumbai. A close-knit community, Bengalis are a warm academic people with great veneration for art and culture. While Marwaris have lived for generations among Kolkata's older inhabitants, they have never been welcomed into its folds with open arms. Kolkata had historically enjoyed being the pampered child of the British Raj. It was once the pride of the empire, one of the most bustling cities between Aden and Singapore, supposedly second to only London within the British Empire. Once the British left, it was the Marwaris that helped Kolkata maintain its economy and egged it on towards becoming the prosperous urban agglomeration that it is today.

In spite of the Marwaris' enormous contribution towards the prosperity of the city, many would still say that Bengalis in Kolkata have never been able to see eye to eye with them. Their lifestyles and ideologies have been too dissimilar to blend together easily, like a film of oil slowly spreading over fresh water. Where the Bengalis love their fish, most Marwaris follow a strictly vegetarian diet. Traditionally, being supporters of trade and commerce, Marwaris have been oriented to the right and hence been known to be anti-left politically, whereas the majority of the Bengalis are staunch leftists. This brings a huge rift in daily beliefs of how the government should run, how much education children should receive, what the price of basic necessities should be and the very definition of work ethics. To top it all off, being a highly cultured and educated community of people, Bengalis, since time immemorial, have turned up their noses at businessmen, believing theirs to not be a respectable profession. However, what is amazing is how each community has managed to find its spot in the sun in Kolkata and worked around territories and boundaries to coexist. In fact, although many Marwaris do not speak Bengali, it was amazing to be exposed to numerous market conversations between the two peoples where the Marwari rattled out rates and features of the product in pure Hindi, while the native bargained in fluent Bengali and yet they made reasonable deals!

After having invested fifty years of their lives and business in Kolkata, the Haldiram family are still considered outsiders. Prabhu reckons that this dynamic had played a huge part in shaping his personality and beliefs. 'Kolkata has been a very difficult city for us to settle down in. We have faced obstacles at every turn, from union strikes to unreasonable land laws. It has been one uphill climb,' he said. Some hesitation later, as if making up his mind to share a secret with me, he ruefully added, 'My father once told me that it had been a huge mistake for us to move here. Our development was stunted at every stage and it was only in the '90s, forty years after we had moved here, that we could grow at a fairly exciting pace.'

West Bengal has historically been a communist state and there has always been a huge value placed on labour conditions. Given the slightest of reasons, the union would go on long strikes, forcing businessmen to pay them more or offer them more lenient working hours under the threat of walking out on them while letting the business sink into the ground. 'It was terrible,' confirmed Prabhu. 'The union of workers would go on strike and surround the house of the businessman, making heavy demands. There would be hundreds of them, almost making someone prisoner in their own home. It was a terrifying experience—the imminent threat of violence, added to the helplessness of losing one's livelihood.' A close friend added, 'The police never stepped up to help those locked in. Even today, the unions have the might and power to burn the home of a businessman and get away with it.'

The Agarwals faced their first major union strike in 1975. The traumatic experience left Prabhu marred for life, unable to ever trust workers from that day forward. He began to take a tough approach with his workforce ever since and strongly believes that only might can defeat might.

'That year, the workers shut down our home for two whole days. It sounds like a short period of time, but our electricity lines were cut, our telephone lines were disabled and all access to the outside world had been snapped,' said Mahesh. The house was surrounded by a mob of workers chanting their demands, yelling their threats and creating a deep well of terror in the minds of their temporary prisoners. Their cries in Bengali ripped into the silent night, creating a sense of danger and doom:

'The bosses drink our blood.'
'They make us slog and enjoy a lavish life of luxuries themselves!'
'They commit murderous atrocities.'
'Kill the bosses, bend them to our will.'
'Give us our money, give us shorter hours.'

Imagine being stuck in a lone house surrounded by a growing mob of workers, holding flaming torches and getting more and more passionately involved in their demands by the minute. The debilitating experience left the family reeling for months and years to come.

'We screamed for the police to help us, and they simply shook their head and remained silent. I was seventeen years old. It was a huge wake-up call. Nobody, not even the law, would come to your aid in such situations.'

The incident was devastating for Rameshwarlal and his sons even more than usual because up until then they had only experienced an upward movement of their business, their wealth and social standing. They had begun to view all of that security as power and the moment they realized that the workers could not simply be ordered to accept certain directions, the rules of the game changed. New perspectives and skills had to be deployed to deal with this new challenge. The father, who had a calm personality, found the shift to being a diplomatic negotiator easier than his hot-blooded son, Prabhu, who has been rumoured to lose his cool on occasion. Mahesh narrated, 'One night all the workers walked out of the factory and refused to come back in to work. Prabhu has occasionally been known to explode into a nasty temper and that evening he got into a physical fight with one of the workers. Even after we were boycotted, my father remained calm and collected. I don't remember him giving my brother a hard time about it.'

However, in spite of having a volatile personality, Prabhu seems to have grown into a more mature leader, which was evident in the way he spoke to his staff and workers during my visit to the Singur factory—with respect and professionalism. He seems to have also adopted several strategies to keep his labourers happy. The fifty-seven-year old businessman has built multistorey living quarters for his labourers with an air-conditioned kitchen area on the ground floor, serving three free meals a day. With the unions extremely strong in Kolkata, the cost of labour is higher than in most other states. Add to that, if the attrition of workers is high, the company endures greater expenses trying to find new workers, wasting precious production time when understaffed and training the new recruits. Prabhu learnt to dole out the carrot or the stick, as the situation required. Today, he offers his workers eight-hour shifts and excellent healthcare benefits while focusing on discovering other innovative ways to reduce costs.

It was almost impossible to read Prabhu. The stories continually contradicted each other, making it very difficult to clearly understand and categorize the man. For example, a close relative depicted him as an anti-hero of the 1970s Bollywood films. Allegedly, there was one time when a group of hooligans ate a load of sweets at his showroom and then refused to pay up. Remember how Shiv Kishan experienced similar challenges in Nagpur? Similar stories but the ending in this case was completely different. Prabhu instantly rallied his 300–350 workers to come with him and surround the showroom with the hooligans inside. He apparently took centre position, reassuring his men that he would take all responsibility and bullied the hooligans into leaving. There are rumours of some violence but apparently the police wrote the report in his favour due to the overall sentiment of the situation. The man was bold and refused to back down or take meek action because the neighbours could be watching. He immediately jumped up and took charge to protect his business. Notice how it never occurred to him to ask for help from the police. This instinctive distrust of the forces since the union incident in 1975 led to some of the most testing times later in his life.

On the one hand, Prabhu is unafraid of violence. Yet, on the other hand, he can demonstrate great patience and leadership. During my visit to Singur, a worker made the mistake of his career! One of the best-selling sweets of Haldiram's Prabhuji was kaju katli, a close cousin of the famous kaju barfi. The usual recipe had cardamom in it; however, Prabhu had found that cardamom, when replaced with saffron, makes for an even more delectable dessert. Saffron is also one of the most expensive of Indian spices. With the addition of just one more ingredient, his was going to be a premium selling sweet. He ordered the workers to make the sweet with the new ingredient and production was in play. One of the workers ended up using both cardamom and saffron as the two raw materials were next to his workstation and he had obviously missed the memo. Hundreds of tonnes of the product had been ruined and had to be disposed of. A moment of silence settled over the factory floor after the first horrified exclamation from Prabhu. I was expecting an outrage of psychedelic proportions to follow. However, Prabhu simply gave the worker a slap on the wrist, asking him questions to get a thorough understanding of what had gone wrong and coolly asked the supervisor to ensure that no bags of cardamom were kept near the kaju katli work stations again. His managerial authority and cool thinking were impressive, and the workers could continue working in a positive frame of mind. However, Prabhu had also learnt to curb his anger and change the way he dealt with workers after several accounts of boycotts and walkouts. Newspaper reports claim he had several legal complaints against him for dealing with workers in an abusive manner and had also been arrested in the past for allegedly assaulting a customer once.[4] With the union strong, and his reputation going against him, several relatives claim that he has had to mend his ways over the years in order to survive Kolkata's unique socio-economic situation.

'The incident with the union workers in 1975 slowed down our growth. We had built a second small factory on Braman Road in 1970 and did not even try to expand beyond that for the next 25 years. While we organically opened a few more showrooms, it was only in 1991 that things changed for the better when the communist government fell and liberalization swept the nation. Since then workers have been more cooperative,' said Prabhu.

However, before they could ride that wave of expansion, tragedy and devastation hit the family with double the intensity. Rameshwarlal had four sons—the eldest, Prabhu Agarwal, followed by Ravi Agarwal, Mahesh Agarwal and Ashok Agarwal. On 21 May 1991, on the same day that the country was reeling after the death of its beloved prime minister, Rajiv Gandhi, the Agarwals in Kolkata were dealing with great sorrow of their own. Ravi Agarwal passed away in a tragic car accident in Bikaner. He and his wife, Shobha Devi Agarwal, had been visiting Shiv Ratan Agarwal in his home and along with their two children, were driving to a nearby temple from his place. The specifics of the story are a little hazy; however, the car hit a rough spot, did a 360-degree flip and landed upside down with great force several feet away from where it had first hit trouble. Husband and wife had been sitting in front and reportedly, while Ravi Agarwal died instantly, his wife survived, albeit with severe injuries.

---

[4] 'See No Evil in Burrabazar', *Tehelka*, 20 February 2010. http://www.tehelka.com/2010/02/see-no-evil-in-burrabazar/.

The two kids and the driver, who were sitting in the back seat, had apparently been thrown out, bounced off the road into nearby shrubbery and escaped death.

The four brothers had been very close and it was a huge loss for the family. However, according to Poonam Chand, Prabhu's uncle, in the weeks prior to his death, Ravi had approached Manoharlal in Delhi about setting up a shop of his own there. Rumours spread about a distance that had slowly cultivated between the two brothers, Prabhu and Ravi, and that the latter had felt inclined to leave the family grounds for newer pastures. However, other rumours explain Ravi's move as a plan sanctioned by all of Rameshwarlal's sons. While Manoharlal had helped Ravi purchase a shop in Delhi, he had requested that they start a business in Delhi under another name, perhaps an extension to the Haldiram name but adding Kolkata to it in order to help differentiate between the two brands. Ravi had agreed, making their move to Delhi an imminent possibility. However, days later he had tragically passed away in his twenties, leaving his elder brother Prabhu in charge of further conversations about expanding into Delhi.

Even before the brothers could come to terms with what had happened to Ravi and his wife, their father and mentor, Rameshwarlal, died a natural death, a couple of days later, on 23 May 1991. The months following the losses were filled with grief and confusion. Emotions were running high and the family was put through a very testing time. Rameshwarlal had been the central beam that held them all together and with him gone, the rest of the building began giving way. The official story is that once their father died, the brothers each decided that running different businesses might be the best path to success and split the enterprise five ways. A part each for each of the brothers and a fifth part for their mother, Kamala Devi.

'My brother and father died in the same year. There was a lot for us to deal with emotionally. We then separated and went our own ways with the business,' said Mahesh. Almost anticipating my next question, he continued, 'There are positives and negatives of staying together. If everyone has the same point of view, then it makes sense to stay together. However, if your core views are not similar, then it is better to separate.' He turned even more philosophical when he added, 'to develop a country it is important to have different states. This helps all areas to develop faster as they receive more focused attention.'

There seems to almost be a sort of defiance that Rameshwarlal's sons exhibit when supporting their decisions to separate from each other and run separate business units. Perhaps because they could find no common ground to work together or perhaps because egos came in the way of the enterprise, they use the 'by separating, we could grow with focus' argument as a justification for their past actions. This split conversely has restricted them from ever being able to get an initial public offering (IPO) as assets and finances need to be in shape and declared before a company can go public. In addition to that, the Haldiram brand name remains an issue, as the brothers will need to get trademarked brand names so as to make sure the public can easily distinguish between the various companies. This has also enhanced their vulnerability in terms of individual assets as the brand divisions seem to be more verbal rather than on paper. The unspoken question remains, had they truly been running business units under the same umbrella corporation, sharing capital and resources, would they have been an even stronger global brand to reckon with?

While Mahesh insists that the split happened simply because it made more business sense, on 10 February 2010, a close confidante of Mahesh told the *Telegraph* otherwise, 'We had split from Prabhu in the late 1990s as he tried to channelize money into risky ventures like real estate.'[5] Even as the brothers vocally align themselves with each other and stand together in unity in the public eye, close family members believe that the acrimony between them due to real estate issues has only intensified over time.

With the separation finalized in 1991, the four brothers were free to pursue their goals independently, and they did. Prabhu began putting plans in motion to expand his part of the business in Kolkata. While his father was alive, they had already begun distributing packets of their namkeen to retail outlets and small shops. The first step was to build strong relationships with carrying and forwarding (C&F) agents, super-stockists and channel distributors. C&F agents act as caretakers of the goods until distributors or wholesalers made a demand. They receive a commission based on goods sold and help mediate between the manufacturers of goods and the chain of distribution. A super-stockist is a kind of C&F agent that has some infrastructure in the form of a warehouse, manpower and service vehicles in order to transport a required amount of goods to a distributor at an agreed commission. These are all points of transit between the actual manufacturer and the retailer where the customer

[5] 'Split Is Showing in Bhujia Empire', *Telegraph*, 10 February 2010. http://www.telegraphindia.com/1100210/jsp/calcutta/story_12086326.jsp.

can purchase the products. A strong distribution network in addition to a popular brand helped reduce commissions and ensured shelf space at multiple retailers. Prabhu spent years strengthening relationships with distributors and expanding his network. Today, due to their greater bargaining power, they pay some of the smallest commissions in the industry: 2 per cent to all C&F agents and 7 per cent to channel distributors. They leverage their strong network to distribute nationwide as well as export internationally.

With distribution picking up pace, the demand for snacks went up tremendously. When Ashok, the youngest of Rameshwarlal's sons moved to Delhi, Prabhu's main competitor in Kolkata remained his cool-headed, second brother, Mahesh. Prabhu began selling under the additional brand name Haldiram's Prabhuji while Mahesh maintained a showroom with the brand name Haldiram. Newspapers abound with stories on how they launched several price wars against each other, yet maintained their familial bonds in spite of running competing businesses. Other family brands such as Bhikharam Chandmal run by Poonam Chand and his son Ashish Agarwal in Kolkata came a distant third to the Haldiram brands. According to Anchal Agarwal, Mahesh's eldest daughter, now pursuing her PhD in electronics at the University of California in Santa Barbara, her mother always said that out of the four brothers, Prabhu had the keenest business sense. In spite of his unpredictable personality, he seemed to have a nose for lucrative opportunities and constantly endeavoured to grow the business.

In 1994, Prabhu Agarwal bought the building near the Netaji Subhash Chandra Bose airport in Kolkata that now hosts his corporate offices. This was developed with an artistic charm unique to Prabhu. The location was priceless and hundreds of travellers would stop by his showroom for a meal before or after their journey. People bought sweet packs and snack packs as gifts from the showroom, sending demand soaring through the roof. In 2005, in order to keep up with the demand, Prabhu invested in land in Alampur on the outskirts of Kolkata and began building factories for *soan papadi*, a popular dessert, as well as other snacks. 'With the factory established, our production went up more than twenty times in the following years,' said Prabhu. 'We have never had any stockpiling issues— never a worry about goods wasting away in a godown since the demand here is unquenchable. We always sell out our goods within a couple of months at the most. And what doesn't get sold immediately sells like hot cakes during major festivals like Diwali and Holi.' The brothers claim that sales during the major festivals make up for any drought periods. Production is planned to accommodate the higher demands during those times. For example, during Baisakhi, the festival of spring, 5000 kilos of sweets are sold per day, as against 2000 kilos per week during the regular season. Demand goes up from 35,000 kilos a week to almost 20,00,000 kilos!

The same logic applies to competition between brothers using similar brand names in the same region. While there is some amount of cannibalization, according to Poonam Chand, 'The market is so huge that we aren't quite eating into each other's share yet. However, when the market becomes more saturated, and several more of the non-branded players become branded, then the brand name will have incredible value. Already there are brand wars in cities where it matters.'

Haldiram's Prabhuji won the hearts and minds of customers across West Bengal. To keep up with ever-increasing demand, Prabhu continued to expand and build more factories. In 2010, production began in the Singur factory, again tripling their production and sales. Distribution made the brand stronger and soon they were miles ahead of the rest of the snacks brands in West Bengal. 'Our brand has huge mileage with the people. People trust our quality and our word. I've seen other shopkeepers trying to sell eggless cakes crumble under the suspicious eyes of customers who would not believe them. However, when Haldiram's Prabhuji claims to be selling eggless cakes, the same aunties and teachers and all vegetarians come in flocks to buy our product. That is our heritage.'

His confidence might have had some semblance of truth in it as I watched a young couple pack and buy kilos of *chhole* (spicy chickpeas) in airtight packages for their trip to the United States later that night. 'It's Haldiram's, not just another roadside shop! They always have great quality. The seal is airtight and it should hold through the journey to the US. We do this every year when we come.'

Exports currently form 10 per cent of Prabhu's total sales. While India's older population grew up on Haldiram's and has always been loyal to the brand, it is currently facing intense competition from international companies such as PepsiCo, Britannia and ITC in the snacks and crisps market for teenagers and kids. While these international brands have only dabbled in the traditional snacks market, they are becoming popular with Western-flavoured snacks such as crisps. However, Prabhu sees it as an important next step to introduce snack lines that will compete directly with these global brands and provide kids with snacks that appeal to their Indian tastes. He plans to bring in new lines of chips and snacks, like Kurkure, that will tap into the traditional Indian namkeen flavours and capture the youth. The testing teams have been working on innovation and the team is ready to launch a full-blown product line for this young demographic.

Unlike the units in Bikaner and Nagpur, Prabhu has stepped into the modern world of marketing with an open mind and an even more open pocket. With a planned budget of ₹100 crore set aside just for advertising and promotions in 2016, Prabhu claims to have taken the next big step towards actively marketing to a wider audience. Prabhu plans to wield the media as his next weapon of choice. His strategy seems to be completely opposite to that of the Delhi brand, which is currently strategically focusing on strengthening their distribution networks while actively acquiring companies with product lines that will help them reach out to the new demographics. So far, both the Delhi and Kolkata brands have largely depended on word of mouth marketing and distribution. In fact all of their in-house marketing teams are actually performing the functions of distribution! However, working on promotional media campaigns will be a bold new step for Prabhu in order to bring the brand a greater level of awareness and followership. However, the Delhi guys point out that they are pretty well known across India. Pankaj Agarwal said, 'I don't think the matter is whether they know about us, but more about whether we can reach every customer in even the most remote parts of the country.' There are a million different strategies to success, and these tiny differences in opinion demonstrate just that.

With production soaring through the roof, Prabhu also established warehouses that could stockpile between 10–15 lakh kilos of product. Many of these storages were also refrigerated to ensure food was kept fresh and healthy before being shipped for distribution. With greater distribution capabilities, Prabhu realized the extra costs that came with running showrooms. Even before Rameshwarlal died, Prabhu had worked with him to start a franchise operation where they would stock Haldiram goods at a franchise location, and the shopkeeper would pay them a franchise fee for stocking and selling their products. With increased production capacities, franchises popped up across the city like shrubs in spring! Between the two brothers, they now have over fifty franchise outlets across the city. While the franchises hold most of the dry snacks and sweets, Prabhu constantly strives to find ways to reduce costs within the showroom without compromising on quality.

Time is money, and in most back-of-the-house activities, it truly is! The amount of time it takes to make a dish in the showroom and serve it to the customer costs them one extra customer that could have been seated if their previous customer had received the food earlier. To tackle this operational bottleneck, Prabhu started experimenting with frozen foods. I was lucky to have met with him the month before the actual launch. The entrepreneur had implemented the ingenious idea that if food was semi-cooked, packaged and frozen in the factories and then delivered to the restaurants, the cooking staff simply needed to reheat enough for that day, making the process of cooking much quicker, thereby opening up the showroom for greater seating. Months of experimentation had led them to ensure that the quality of the product still met original standards.

Prabhu confirmed that studies in the West also showed that frozen foods tended to retain the nutritional content of fresh foods if frozen immediately.

I was treated to a lunch of idli and sambhar at the restaurant. Immediately after I had delivered a genuine compliment— 'These idlis are actually better than the ones my mom makes at home'—he told me that they were actually part of his frozen foods menu. Mind you, I'm a Tamilian and my mother is a fantastic cook! While he is not the only Haldiram owner to be producing frozen packaged goods, his single-minded desire to cut costs and make a profit drove him to be innovative in all spheres of business operations. These frozen foods have allowed Prabhu to fearlessly franchise restaurants as well. While Pankaj Agarwal, the scion of the much larger Delhi business, expressed his hesitation towards franchises, Prabhu has ensured that their frozen foods could be served at these restaurants, ensuring consistency in quality and presentation. The Delhi folks have put expanding the business into franchises on the back-burner due to considerations of consistency. They claim that once their own business is fully under control and processes have been established, only then can they start franchises, teach protocols and extend training. Pankaj claims, 'The credibility of the brand is above everything else. We will not enter franchising because we believe we do not yet have the proper processes in place to ensure that it translates just as well into the original.'

The restaurant part of the business for Haldiram Bhujiawala in Kolkata began only in 1997. Since then, the public has been crazy about the Haldiram's Prabhuji quick-serve menus. In just fifteen years, their total products displayed within showrooms and offered at restaurants have gone up to 400 different varieties.

The restaurants quickly became vehicles for promotional PR, helping to showcase different kinds of sweets and snacks, leveraging people's growing affinity with the brand which helped the business gain greater momentum in its distribution activities. Even while churning out innovation, Prabhu and his team continually follow their deceased grandfather's lesson of 'the Customer is God'. New products are tested in the form of samples before they are introduced in the market. The restaurants make customers feel extra special. According to Dhiru Banerjee, Prabhu's closest friend and a Bengali actor, 'the waiters have been trained to put the customers' needs first. If a customer complains about something in the food, the waiters have been specifically told to quietly take the plate away and offer the customer a new one, sans any questions.' Perhaps this is a consequence of previous complaints against Prabhu and his treatment of customers. However, the restaurants undoubtedly enjoy a large patronage of loyalists, helping them hit their revenue targets more effectively.

'We want to double our growth every year for at least the next ten years. That's the ambition and the plan,' said Prabhu, sitting behind his massive desk. He, like all his brothers and cousins, strongly believes that packaging played a major role in the success of the brands. 'You can take this in writing that Prabhu Agarwal said it—branding and packaging are the two most important reasons behind our success,' he said emphatically, his eyes shining with passion. 'In Bengal, back in the day, soan papadi used to be sold loose. It had a shelf life of two to four days and customers only bought a few pieces of it at a time for fear of it going bad. These sweets were all considered perishables once upon a time. However now, with triple, quadruple and five-layer sophisticated packaging, our products have a shelf life of six to eight months and are being exported to the United States, Australia, Singapore, United Kingdom, etc. A product that sold about 50 kilos a day, now has a daily production of one lakh kilos and garners recognition across the globe.' Over two decades ago, this shelf life, this production capacity and the concept of exporting to foreign countries would have felt like a far-fetched fantasy to the family. Yet today, in spite of their extremely humble roots, it wears the glowing halo of reality.

At annual revenues of over ₹500 crore, Prabhu ranks third in terms of annual revenues after the Delhi and Nagpur establishments. Operating from a single state, he has pushed almost every possible boundary on his way to becoming one of Kolkata's most successful businessmen.

Ambition, according to his brother Mahesh, has been Prabhu's greatest strength and also his greatest weakness. It pushed him beyond the black-and-white edges of legality, overlooking the fact that ambition without moral margins could lead him down a very dark path. In his desire to expand and pursue fame, wealth and power, Prabhu papered over several ethical cracks to the point where even if he wanted to, he could no longer retreat. Yet, while several parties including the law hold him responsible, the lines of the story blur as a few family members wonder if he actually went the distance he was accused of going. They didn't believe that he was capable of such dark acts.

## Self-perpetuating Prophecy

The Singur factory, on the outskirts of Kolkata, was built on thirty acres of gently meandering farmland. Prabhu Agarwal is the proud owner of most of this estate, except for a few odd small plots of land that stand out like missing pieces of a gigantic jigsaw puzzle. In spite of the intense humidity in June, he insisted on taking me on a walking tour across his estate, eager to show off his automated systems and machinery. Sweat dripping down the side of his face, he hobbled along with a walking stick—which he had to use after sustaining a hip injury while playing catch with his eight-year-old grandson the previous day. Smilingly, he shrugged off his discomfort, saying, 'Playing with my grandchildren is one of the greatest joys of this life.'

We walked along some fresh construction sites where new factory buildings were coming up, while he complained about the bazillion legal hurdles that entrepreneurs faced in West Bengal. Pointing to one of the plots of land that did not belong to him, he complained about how the political leaning of the then government made a huge impact on the lives of the people, especially on the entrepreneurs in West Bengal. From 1977 to 2011, the state was headed by a CPM-led Left Front government that supported the cause of unions to a point that it put the lives of entrepreneurs in danger. Even as the current chief minister, Trinamool leader Mamta Banerjee's government has demonstrated less tolerance towards corporate hegemony.

'It has taken me years to buy this land. Piece by piece, we (my sons and I) bought plots from the farmers to build this estate. There were at least a handful of farmers who remained stubborn in the face of pressure and monetary perks. They gave in eventually when the need for immediate cash was great, but up until then, we had to put up with odd pieces of unusable land in the site of our factory buildings,' said a visibly irritated Prabhu Agarwal.

It takes resolve and strength of conviction to hold on to a lonely farm plot when surrounded by acres of industrial land and hostile neighbours. The farmers choose to hold their ground, perhaps out of sentimentality to preserve their ancestral lands or hoping to win a larger sum of money for it before caving in to entrepreneurial ambition.

Under the previous two chief ministers, Jyoti Basu and Buddhadeb Bhattacharya, the government worked under what was called the Land Acquisition Act of 1894 had been instated under the British Raj. According to Prabhu, 'In the '90s, the government would intervene and help us acquire land. If the land was owned by a hundred farmers and only ninety of them wished to sell, the government had the right to evict them, buy the land and send all the farmers cheques as compensation. Some industrialists purchased land privately and if even one farmer out of a hundred refused to sell, the government would step in and help ease the process. However, the current government has refused to step in.' There was anguish in his eyes and I realized he must be making a case for his former alleged illegal land deals. Stepping over a ditch, we stood at the edge of a farmer's plot, staring past the barbwire-fencing at the five sheep grazing on the wild grass.

'Now the farmers are selling only one at a time. It takes months, sometimes even years to convince each famer to sell. I bought a 100-acre piece of land but only thirty acres is currently mine. I have a while to go before I convince the rest of the farmers to sell,' he said. That took me by surprise. I wondered how that could even work. To which he replied, 'You cannot buy land without getting permission from the government. And, even after having the permission, you need to buy it individually from the famer or else risk having the land confiscated.'

Prabhu's drive and desire to grow his empire was almost intoxicating but it was also surprising to see his lack of empathy for those displaced or his inherent disregard for the law. He thinks his only crime here has been in working with a single-minded focus on growing his business and a willingness to break a few rules to do so. His twenty-five-year-old niece Anchal Agarwal said later, with a cynicism uncharacteristic of her age, 'In a country like India with all its bureaucratic hurdles, I feel that if someone has achieved something, they have bent some rules along the way. It's almost impossible to achieve success in the business world without doing at least something you shouldn't.' There is an odd sort of acceptance within the business community in India, especially amongst the Marwaris of Kolkata, that certain deviant steps have to be taken in order to succeed. Businessmen are considered tougher than most in the community because they have had to follow through on decisions that most people would find uncomfortable taking. However, Anchal added a caveat, 'The question is, where will you draw the line?'

It is well known that two and a half decades ago, Rameshwarlal and his sons' acquisition of huge land on VIP Road had been allegedly made possible only because of help from the then CPM leader Subhash Chakraborty who it is said had brokered a deal at a very low rate for them.[6] Rumours abound that this triggered a severe clash between the CPM and Congress members in the state assembly. Allegedly, Chakraborty helped

---

[6] 'See No Evil in Burrabazar', *Tehelka*, 20 February 2010. http://www.tehelka.com/2010/02/see-no-evil-in-burrabazar/?singlepage=1.

Prabhu acquire multiple pieces of land thereafter, including for his massive Chowringee store. While articles from the *Indian Express* place Prabhu as a close friend of the then CM Jyoti Basu, they claim that he could never get along with CM Buddhadeb Bhattacharya in quite the same way. Then Congressman Nirbed Roy (now a part of Trinamool Congress) once told *Tehelka*, 'He [Prabhu] rarely followed the law of the land.'[7]

Prabhu learnt early on that money was power and having met multiple corrupt officials over the course of his career, his dogmas only grew stronger. It is said that his first move during negotiations was always to offer the opposing party a lucrative deal. If that didn't work, he allegedly would resort to force and violence in order to scare them into subservience. He says that greed and fear are omnipresent weaknesses in all human beings regardless of their station or position and he had perfected the art of using them to his advantage. Little did he know that he would one day be caught at his game and that even tycoons could end up behind bars.

He once barged into West Bengal's fire minster Pratim Chatterjee's office determined to employ his first strategy: buy the adversary. Chatterjee is recorded telling the *Indian Express*, 'I received several complaints that the manufacturing unit of Prabhu's Haldiram's was violating all fire norms. So I shut down the unit. A few days after his manufacturing unit on VIP Road was sealed, Agarwal barged into my office and told me that he had an order from a foreign country and a consignment worth ₹38 crore needed to be delivered to Italy

---

[7] 'See No Evil in Burrabazar', *Tehelka*, 20 February 2010. http://www.tehelka.com/2010/02/see-no-evil-in-burrabazar/.

within a couple of weeks. I refused to allow him to open the factory kitchens. He told me that everyone has a price and asked me what was my price. I threw him out of my office!'[8] Allegedly, according to *Tehelka*'s records, around the same time, Prabhu unleashed his band of brutes on an unsuspecting police team. The article suggests that these troublemakers often lunched at his outlets, awaiting orders to 'rough up his adversaries'. The grapevine has it that they smashed the police jeep, thwarting the officers' investigation into his operations, particularly into how his generators were running, violating fire laws. He was locked in a solitary cell for twenty days, during which he is said to have 'bribed the police with ₹10,000 per day to avoid harsh questioning'.[9] In spite of being stonewalled and shamed by a politician in addition to having spent time in jail, Prabhu Agarwal didn't take this incident as a cue to change his ways. He had spent too many hard years trying to nurture his business, and such incidents were only tiny obstacles to him—obstacles that forced him to discover more creative ways of circumventing the rules.

A momentary conversation shared between him and Poonam Chand several years ago exemplifies his resilient nature: 'Once, after a long day at work, Prabhu and I were sharing a bottle of rum between us. I remember complaining to him about the fact that we worked so hard, yet our products didn't sell as much. I carried on, going down the winding path towards "life is so unfair". Finally, Prabhu looked at me and replied rather

---

[8] 'The Boss & His Hit-man', *Indian Express*, 1 February 2010. http://archive.indianexpress.com/news/the-boss---his-hitman/573839/.

[9] 'See No Evil in Burrabazar', *Tehelka*, 20 February 2010. http://www.tehelka.com/2010/02/see-no-evil-in-burrabazar/?singlepage=1.

intensely, "If a man truly desires, he can squeeze water from stone." ' While this dialogue has 'Rajnikanth folklore' written all over it, it certainly renders a glimpse into a man who has been determined to achieve his goals and follow his ambitions taking on all odds.

Nobody has ever been able to come up with any concrete answer to the age-old question of nature versus nurture, just like the chicken-and-egg conundrum. Was it the corrupt business practices in the real estate industry in Kolkata that forced Prabhu to follow that path? Or was it because of his personality that he had chosen the path of alleged extortion or violence? While both could have played a major role in the making of his persona, it is clear that circumstances pushed him along his course.

Kolkata, a sprawling, bustling city, has grown significantly to be ranked among India's biggest cities—while its population has exploded to over 13 million, the city has simply not been able to expand to create suburbs at a fast-enough pace to accommodate its citizens. In the central business areas of Kolkata, mainly Burrabazaar and the Posta region, space is a highly precious commodity. A businessman within the area says that even a small six-by-six-foot shop could churn out business worth crores.

Space is money in Kolkata and if a businessman wants to expand, he needs to capture more space. Therein lies the problem. According to a local policeman, muscle power and money are the only two languages that make headway in these busy, cut-throat markets. Both are used to grab rival shops, and over the decades have given rise to *supari*, or contract killing, who for a quick buck have only been too willing to intervene in business disputes and force solutions on weaker parties. An *Indian Express*[10] article points to police records that indicate an average of 100 cases of extortion and complaints of financial irregularities filed at the Burrabazaar and Posta police stations on a monthly basis. Reportedly, the area runs on an intoxicating mix of extortion and terror. It was in the midst of this war for real estate that Burrabazaar's very own don, Gopal Tiwari, was born. He was dreaded in the area and worked with several business hot shots and real estate magnates to pressurize small shopkeepers to sell. Allegedly, Gopal Tiwari led Prabhu Agarwal's team for clandestine operations and the two of them had been working together for several years.[11]

It is within this very ecosystem that Prabhu Agarwal set out to establish his empire. However, family members seem to believe that other levers played a greater role in Prabhu's trajectory than just the circumstances he was born in. 'Prabhu was a part of the older generation. They never even went to college. In fact I don't believe any of my uncles have ever even read a book! Whatever they learnt in life, they learnt in the shop, while dealing with customers, dealers, contractors and suppliers. Life taught them how to negotiate successfully and come out the winner in any situation. For them, violence was never wrong. They had learnt to fight for what they believed in. Bribery or fear tactics were just that—tactics.' In Anchal's words lie the truth of the indigenous business community in India. Uneducated, and with an overwhelming lack of capital,

---

[10] 'The Boss & His Hit-man', *Indian Express*, 1 February 2010. http://archive.indianexpress.com/news/the-boss---his-hitman/573839/.
[11] Ibid.

the business class learnt to fend for itself. They stood on their own two feet to build their business and feed their families. Abetted by a lack of strict policing and a burgeoning desire to escape poverty, these businessmen fought for what they believed in—success achieved by hook or crook. This was their credo, something to be proud of.

Moreover, Prabhu had also been strongly influenced by his father. 'Rameshwarlal had ingrained in his son a philosophy to never fear the uniform. He had trained his son to slap a guy first and deal with the rest later. The father–son duo got out of several scrapes in this way. After Prabhu had caused trouble, the police would come to take him away and then Rameshwarlal would play the helpless father, profusely apologizing to the cops for his son's actions, brushing them aside as the actions of a wayward boy. As his was a known name in the community, Rameshwarlal's request would, more often than not, be honoured. This is how Prabhu was taught to be fearless and bold,' said Poonam Chand. Perhaps this is also how Prabhu learnt to intimidate and believe that he could get away with anything. However, his actions and destiny finally caught up with him. After all, as Mahatma Gandhi taught, beliefs become actions, actions become habits, and habits become values that define our destiny.

## Crime and Punishment

*Tehelka*'s article on 20 February 2010 by journalist Gaurav Jain reads: 'On 29 January, in a judgement nobody was expecting, fifty-four-year-old Prabhu was sentenced to life imprisonment by a Kolkata trial court. Going by his beaming face as he stepped out of the jail van, he wasn't expecting it either. He's a man who's always known how to bend the world.'

Everybody, from the business community, policemen, politicians and his family members were shocked by the verdict. While nobody had expected Prabhu to be indicted, they were all quite unsurprised by the crime he was actually accused of committing. In fact, it is said that some businessmen were actually sorry for the poor man's run of 'bad luck'. The same article records a Marwari businessman expressing his sympathies for Prabhu's problems: 'The tea-shop owner should have been more reasonable.' The businessmen of Kolkata had obviously been pampered by a culture where they weren't used to hearing the word 'no'. It seemed outrageous to them that anybody would stand in their path for too long without giving in to their demands. Such behaviour was deemed 'unreasonable', which goes to show how deep the delusions run.

Newspapers across the nation went on a rampage in 2010, covering the story of a snacks baron being meted out justice and having to serve a lifetime in prison. The evidence against Prabhu left the tycoon exposed and vulnerable for perhaps the very first time in his adult life.

Prabhu's reputation preceded him. So he was left out in the cold, with even family members viewing him as the wolf that feigns innocence. It surprised me, the degree of candidness with which some family members talked about him.

His nephew, Ashish Agarwal, heir to Kolkata's Bhikharam Chandmal business, put it bluntly: 'He is a murderer. Check Google and you will get all the information on his court case. He ordered someone to shoot the chaiwala.' When I inquired if this had been absolutely proven, he said, 'Everybody knows. Even he admits that he gave those goons money.' The levels of cynicism differed amongst the family members as they struggled to reconcile these dramatic accusations with the husband, brother, manager and uncle that they had all known for so long. The police reports and the sentence demanding 'life imprisonment', however demonstrate a line of facts, hard to ignore.

Back in 2005, after setting up his first major factory, Prabhu was eager to make his ambitions a reality. Then and now, he wanted to become India's biggest player in the food market. 'I want to be the largest producer and seller of all things food in India,' he said, during our interview in June 2015. To achieve this dream a decade ago, he needed to build a mall in a prime location in Kolkata. With the factory established, he was convinced that production would soar and an outlet to sell all his innovations would take his growth to the next level.

Prabhu already owned two multistoreyed outlets in the heart of Burrabazar, at 7, Jagmohan Mullick Road, and 9, Jagmohan Mullick Road. The plan was to construct an even more impressive mall in the middle of these two buildings. He had begun working with Arun Khandelwal, a giant in the construction industry to make this a reality since 1996. The prize was an existing building at 8, Jagmohan Mullick Road, which they planned to bulldoze; however, a small tea-shop owner's stall stood out like a sore thumb right in front of what would become one-of-a-kind, classy and glamorous food mall.

With enough pressure and clout, Prabhu managed to intimidate the seventy-five-year-old landlord of the building, Chandrawali Singh. Prabhu, at the time, had already begun working with Gopal Tiwari, whose reputation as Burrabazaar's most fearsome don had made him as recognizable a brand as the Haldiram name itself. Allegedly, Arun Khandelwal had introduced Gopal Tiwari to Prabhu. Khandelwal, a mighty baron within the construction industry, hadn't come this far without some questionable actions himself. Construction is an especially shady business in India, with bribes passing in all directions up and down the food chain from small-time construction crew to politicians. One didn't get one's hands on a prime piece of land without first getting them dirty. Khandelwal, by 2005, already had four cases filed against him under the Arms Act.[12] Tiwari, hired by Khandelwal, had a front for supplying construction materials but in reality, his main profession seems to be that of a goon for hire.

Prabhu, being a big boy, was fully aware of the consequences of running with this crowd. Yet, he ran amuck with a sense of immunity and a high that only comes from having gotten away with one too many misdemeanours. With each *Lakshman rekha* crossed into the world of immorality, the concept of right and wrong blurs, helping these businessmen justify their actions to themselves. 'I'm not much worse than the other guy,' becomes the standing argument and so begins the slippery slope towards actions one can never take back, as is evident in Prabhu Agarwal's case. He had multiple signs cautioning him from the path—the twenty days spent in jail after harassing the West Bengal Fire Minister Pratim Chatterjee, the humiliation by a politician and his own brothers pulling away ashamed to be associated too closely with him. Yet, Prabhu found the lure of his ambitions too strong to resist.

---

[12] 'The Boss & His Hit-man', *Indian Express*, 1 February 2010. http://archive.indianexpress.com/news/the-boss---his-hitman/573839/.

The case investigation officer, Uttam Mukherjee, has been recorded telling the *Indian Express* that business was so cut-throat in Burrabazar that it led businessmen to give thugs and goons in the area commissions in order to buy protection or immunity from rivals. According to Mukherjee, 'Almost all businessmen in the area look for protection by paying a commission, and businessmen like Agarwal would all the more require the help of the underworld for clandestine operations.'

Between 1996 and 2005, Prabhu had bought out all the tenants of the building barring one—the tea stall that spoilt the view of the building from the street ahead. As per Kolkata police records, there were originally eight shops on the premises of the building that Prabhu needed to demolish in order to start construction. He succeeded in convincing seven of those tenants to sell their shops, their livelihood, for amounts between ₹1 and 3 lakh each. While these seven owners succumbed to pressure and accepted the pitiable amounts, Satyanarayan Sharma (alias Satyanarayan Thakur) and his nephew Pramod Sharma, owners of the small tea stall, refused to cave in to the powerful tycoon.

A senior police official of the area said, 'One square feet of area here fetches at least ₹10,000–₹15,000. A six-by-six-foot shop area, like the tea stall owned by Pramod Sharma, would at least be worth ₹8 lakh.'[13] While the amount offered to the tea-stall owners was way below the actual worth of their shop, it didn't seem to be the main reason behind their defiance.

---

[13] 'The Boss & His Hit-man', *Indian Express*, 1 February 2010. http://archive.indianexpress.com/news/the-boss---his-hitman/573839/.

Pramod and his family had been running this tea shop for over fifty years, and it seemed to hold great sentimental significance for them aside from being the key source of their income. This is all they had done for over two generations and the thought of selling it was unimaginable for them. Uttam Mukherjee confirms this when he says, 'It has been a family business for Pramod, and his uncles were also involved,' implying the difficulty of taking such a decision.

In the days following the attempted murder when the *Indian Express* caught up with Pramod, he said, '*Hum mar jayenge, lekin apna dukan nahi chorengeye, bade log hum jaise gareeb ko roz marte hai, aise marne se toh achcha hai ki ek baar mar jaye.*'[14] (We will die, but not let go of our shop. These rich people kill us poor people in innumerable small ways every day. It is better to die once and for all than keep dying every moment.)

Passionate, brave and head-strong, Pramod and his uncle Satyanarayan stuck to their guns to the very end, a rare show of courage in an economy where the small fish always cower in fear under the assumption that they will never win. Prabhu had been endeavouring to capture this piece of land for almost ten years and his patience and fortitude were beginning to give way.

In 2005, once Prabhu had won over seven of the eight tenants, he filed a case in the city court against the seventy-five-

---

[14] 'Won't Quit Tea-stall, Says Man Who Stood Up to Snacks Baron', *Indian Express*, 29 January 2010. http://archive.indianexpress.com/news/won-t-quit-teastall-says-man-who-stood-up-to-snacks-baron/572718/.

year-old Chandrawali Singh.[15] The court gave an ejection order to Singh's tenants, and the landlord, being old and tired, quickly gave in to Prabhu's demands. Even after all the tenants left the premises, the Sharmas challenged the ejection order and filed a review petition in the civil court. During the period that the case was pending, Pramod and his uncle could not be thrown off the premises.

'*Aapka bhao kitna hai?*'[16] Prabhu had asked Pramod his 'price' during the initial days and offered him ₹4 lakh for the shop. This famous line was one that Prabhu constantly used, enabling him to achieve most of his desires. However, it did not fly with this highly scrupulous tea-stall owner and his uncle. After their refusal to comply with the court order, a frustrated Prabhu decided that he needed to take more drastic action in order to force them to leave. Things happened pretty fast after that.

On 12 February 2005, an officer of the court was scheduled to survey the site to make sure that all tenants had left the premises. Had that been the case, Prabhu and his developer, Arun Khandelwal, would have been free to demolish the building and start work on their dream project. Desperate to get Pramod and his uncle to leave, Prabhu allegedly let his goons loose on the unsuspecting pair. 'Prabhu had to remove our stall from the area before the officer got there,' said Pramod later.

The then twenty-one-year-old shop owner, Pramod, received his first jolt in a series of shocks to come, that morning.

---

[15] 'See No Evil in Burrabazar', *Tehelka*, 20 February 2010. http://www.tehelka.com/2010/02/see-no-evil-in-burrabazar/?singlepage=1.

[16] 'The Boss & His Hit-man', *Indian Express*, 1 February 2010. http://archive.indianexpress.com/news/the-boss---his-hitman/573839/.

The hired goons completely ransacked the shop, demolishing furniture and décor. According to the papers, when Satyanarayan and a relative, Gopal Thakur, tried to resist, the goons beat them up with bricks and wooden planks. Once the police got there, Pramod assumed that help had finally come and heaved a sigh of relief, frantically crying out for aid. He was, however, shocked when the police captured him and Gopal Thakur and put them in the lock-up instead of the goons for disrupting public peace. Tales of corruption within India's police force are by no means unheard of; they are heartbreaking for the ordinary man to come to terms with the bitter reality that they are on their own, a lesson that Prabhu had learnt much earlier. A lesson that had driven him to leverage money and clout in order to make sure he would always be in the position of power, not weakness.

The experience behind bars did not weaken the young, feisty Pramod. To make sure his threats were taken seriously, Prabhu ordered Satyanarayan to be forcibly taken to Binani Dharamshala at 85 Pathuria Street, a kilometre away from the tea stall. Here, the veteran owner was introduced to Prabhu Agarwal, the business magnate, in all his powerful glory for the first time. Imagine his plight, a sixty-five-year-old humble tea-stall owner with no clout in the world, physically accosted by hooligans, dragged into an unknown vehicle and brought to hear his sentence in the court of this powerful businessman. Just the thought of this kidnapping might be enough to make many men tremble in fear and helplessness. But not Satyanarayan. It seems bravery ran in the bloodline. Arun Khandelwal, Prabhu's developer, allegedly mediated the meeting, and Gopal Tiwari, the don, dramatically opened a briefcase in front of Satyanarayan. The case was filled with cash, a scene typical of the movies. 'It contained ₹4 lakh, I was told. Gopal asked me to accept the money or else prepare to face dire consequences. I refused,'[17] said the principled Satyanarayan.

Allegedly, Prabhu Agarwal then contracted Gopal Tiwari and his men, Manoj Sharma and Rajiv Sonkar, to 'take out' the tea-stall owner. Three days after the kidnapping, the drunken goons drove up to the tea stall in a Hyundai Accent and opened fire at the shop. Newspaper articles refer to this incident as 'a supari or contract kill order that had comically backfired'. The goons, in spite of being called 'expert shooters' in other articles, never hit their mark, leaving their victims alive, though not kicking. Pramod Sharma got shot in his thigh and was seriously injured. He was taken to the Calcutta Medical College and Hospital where the doctors operated on his left leg, leaving him able to walk with a limp all through his life.

In order to avoid suspicion, the team apparently scattered. Gopal Tiwari was captured a couple of months later on 24 May 2005 in Hyderabad by the Kolkata police officers. He allegedly sang like a canary from that point onwards. He admitted that Prabhu Agarwal had paid him ₹2.5 lakh for the job. Based on this information, the police nabbed Prabhu at the Indira Gandhi International Airport in Delhi on 7 June 2005. He was just returning from a business trip in the UK where he had been endeavouring to set up a branch. Handcuffed and humiliated, Prabhu was instantly launched into the national limelight on

---

[17] 'Won't Quit Tea-stall, Says Man Who Stood Up to Snacks Baron', *Indian Express*, 29 January 2010. http://archive.indianexpress.com/news/won-t-quit-teastall-says-man-who-stood-up-to-snacks-baron/572718/.

that day. Police accounts say that it was he who gave up the other three involved parties under duress, namely Arun Khandelwal, Manoj Sharma and Rajiv Sonkar.

All Prabhu's past stories indicate that he had always had some policemen in his pocket. How then did he finally manage to get arrested? Prabhu's uncle, Poonam Chand's perspective, shed some light into the incident. 'I don't know whether he paid the men to do it or whether he sat in the actual vehicle himself. Nonetheless, I've heard that Prabhu as per usual asked the policeman, *"Apka bhao kitna hai?"* and the policeman told him that if Prabhu gave him ₹20 lakh, there won't be any case against him. The cop knew this was one hell of a scrape to get into and that Prabhu was desperate. However, Prabhu was incensed and allegedly retorted, "I keep IPS officers in my pocket for ₹1000." In order to punish him for his arrogance, the policeman said, 'I'll get you tangled in such a case that you will never be able to get out of it for any amount of bail!'" The misfortune continued, as from then on, the player became the played.

Gopal Tiwari was held in prison without bail. Meanwhile, Prabhu and the other three enjoyed restricted freedom while waiting for court proceedings to continue. It took five years for the case to finally be put in front of a judge who took swift and decisive action. While Tiwari had been in the correctional facility, the four others had had five years to nurture hope. All that came crashing down on them when they were taken into custody and declared guilty by Judge Tapan Sen, on 27 January 2010. Two days later, on 29 January 2005, in the fourth fast track court in Kolkata, Judge Tapan Sen sentenced the five of them to 'life imprisonment'.

The silence of the courtroom broke and the walls reverberated as if thunder had struck. The judge is recorded as saying, 'Prabhu Shankar Agarwal, Gopal Tiwari, Arun Khandelwal, Manoj Sharma and Raju Sonkar are sentenced to life imprisonment under Sections 120B (criminal conspiracy) and 307 (attempted murder) of the Indian Penal Code (IPC).' I can bet the silence that followed was only overpowered by the loud strumming of the anxious heartbeats of the accused. A confused and utterly shocked Prabhu Agarwal allegedly asked his lawyer, Alok Pyne, 'How long is a life sentence?'

'Life imprisonment means life term,' said Pyne.

'You mean till death?' inquired Prabhu.

'Yes,' came the curt response.

In all of this, friends and family members claim that Prabhu remained extremely unruffled and self-contained. His usual 'temper' went missing and an uncharacteristic calm had enveloped him. Perhaps the seriousness of his predicament was finally beginning to sink in. It is rumoured that Prabhu said, 'I am innocent. I have over a thousand families to look after which include all my employees.' With bravado he added, 'I will take whatever punishment the court will decide for me.'

People present say that Prabhu Agarwal, Arun Khandelwal, the lawyer Alok Pyne and Prabhu's son, Manish, and Ravi's son, Sharad, huddled together in deep discussion after the verdict. It seemed that they were plotting their next course of action, i.e. taking the matter to a higher court, another action he had made a habit of as can be seen from the court battles for the brand dispute cases.

Before being shipped off to prison, Prabhu supposedly walked over to his wife and said, '*Ek moti sa gaddi, ek accha takia, aur ek kambal bhej dena jail me. Aur tum bilkul fikr mat karo. Hum sab sambhal lenge.'* (Have a thick mattress, a comfortable pillow and a blanket sent to me in jail. And don't worry about a thing. I will take care of all this.) According to family members, while they describe Prabhu as an unpredictable, sometimes violent and tough man, everybody agrees that he had a very soft spot for his wife, Sudha Agarwal.

Sudha Agarwal reportedly remained stoic through the verdict. Gopal Tiwari's wife cried, clutching the metal mesh holding her husband secure. Rajiv Sonkar, in order to calm his family, cracked a joke asking them to deliver a packet of biryani for him in jail. Goodbyes said, the five criminals were sent to Alipore Central Jail, where Prabhu remained for almost the next eight months of his life.

To friends and family, he maintained that he was innocent and he would never have somebody killed. In 2010, a journalist wrote an article about Prabhu's sentence, and his then twenty-year-old niece, Anchal Agarwal, responded in hurt fury. The writer had stated that her defence of Prabhu Agarwal was perhaps a result of her relationship with him. To which, she responded in scathing words. In short, her message said, 'I am his family. I am Mahesh Kumar Agarwal's daughter and Prabhu papa's favourite niece. Right now I am in the US and I am shocked to hear all of this. Having heard what really happened, it hurts to hear the crap people put up on the Internet. Firstly, ponder on why he got a sentence in the first place, even with the system being so corrupt. It's because he did NOT pay any minister and so they turned on him . . . Tiwari himself decided that he wanted to shoot the tea-stall owner. Bade papa had no clue. Or it might have even been that Tiwari and the tea-stall owner were allies. Do you wonder why the tea-stall owner did not die and just got hurt on his foot in spite of the shooters being EXPERT SHOOTERS?'

Today, Anchal Agarwal, older and wiser at twenty-five, admits that perhaps she had been a little misguided. During our conversation, Anchal laughed with obvious embarrassment at her comments online and shook her head at her younger, more gullible self. She confessed that at twenty, she had been unreservedly outraged at the judgment, unable to believe that somebody from her precious family could be sent to jail on a 'criminal charge'. 'I never imagined that my uncles were capable of something like this.' She said that business was never really discussed at home and perhaps at that stage she had naively believed that her family did business the honest way. 'Five years ago, I thought differently. Today, I think he is guilty but not of what he has been charged for. I believe this was a case of trying to scare someone gone horribly wrong. I think businessmen in India use scare tactics all the time, something I've come to accept as I'm older and wiser, and perhaps that is what bade papa was trying to do. He admits to having hired the goons; however, I do not believe that he wanted them to hurt anybody. I think what happened is that some people in the underworld learnt that he wanted to evict the tea-shop owner and they took matters into their own hands and shot at him. I don't think I can say very much more on the subject.'

The eight months in prison prior to getting out on bail were not easy for the Kolkata-based Haldiram tycoon. His friend Dhiru Banerjee sadly tells of Prabhu's depression while being in jail. It was a difficult time for the whole family, especially Prabhu's wife Sudha, and his son, Manish, and nephew, Sharad.

The family watched as their dirty laundry was washed in public, and were unable to hide from prying eyes. Both Prabhu's sons and his brother Mahesh lost a lot of valuable time running around, working with lawyers to get the case appealed in a higher court.

Prabhu was held in a solitary cell fitted with close circuit cameras in the Alipore Central Jail. He was in room 6 of cellblock 14, which was opposite that of Aftab Ansari, the criminal mastermind of the USIS attacks. Family members say that it was a difficult time for all concerned. According to the jail authorities, like ordinary convicts, Prabhu underwent rigorous labour drills. He was allotted the job of a gardener within the jail gardens. Deemed unskilled, his salary was set at the lowest level, i.e. ₹18 per day. The first three months of working were considered probationary, so he began getting paid only after those three months. The rates at the time were ₹21 for semi-skilled labour and ₹25 for highly skilled labourers. Prabhu apparently didn't make the cut for the higher salaries. Dhiru Banerjee says that Prabhu found some respite by escaping into the world of arts. 'It was a very difficult time for him and the family. Sometimes he would get depressed. However, he has always been culturally inclined, supporting the local Kolkata film and theatre industry in whatever way he could. Once he puts his mind to something, he learns very fast. In fact, he learnt how to paint during his time in jail.' Prabhu apparently took painting classes in jail where he made an oil painting of his eight-year-old grandson with just a small passport-size photograph of the boy to serve as his guide.

When asked about the attempted murder, Prabhu became very prickly. He refused to answer my questions and almost lost his cool. He curtly told me off. 'You shouldn't be asking personal questions like these,' came his terse reply. I have to admit, I cowered and pushed no further. However, he did unwrap the painting he had made of his grandson with great joy and pride, asking me to compare the painting with the photo, which I must admit was almost identical. He confessed that the painting had been the only thing to bring him rare moments of solace when everything around had gone dark and that was all he said about the subject. For a man out on bail, with pending appeals in the court, it would have been ideal for him to share his perspective on the incident, to voice his side of the story; an opportunity to perhaps defend himself or shed light on his own innocence. Prabhu, ironically, seems to have closed all doors to this particular discussion.

His brother Mahesh tried to support him as much as he could and to not let the incident affect the family. Mahesh's and Prabhu's sons appealed in the Kolkata High Court right after the fast track court judgment, and almost instantly received a rejection. However, in late September 2010, the Supreme Court granted Prabhu bail under the condition that he would not leave the country until his case was resolved. In spite of the brothers' seemingly united front, people close to both Mahesh and Prabhu commented on how they had begun to drift apart even before that point. When asked about the court case, Mahesh said, 'It is a process that I don't like to think about very much. I feel that everything that happened was wrong and that when a man impulsively commits actions out of avarice and selfishness, it ultimately causes difficulties for him. Even if a person commits a negative action believing that it is indeed right, ultimately that act when done with impure intentions, will never bear good results.' While Mahesh had helped his brother by doing the legal rounds, he somehow couldn't get himself to align with him on his actions and philosophy. The judgment had shaken their world and while they had already split the business before all this had truly begun, they were at that point beginning to see major fissures within the internal structure of the family itself.

To that effect, in another conversation, Anchal said, 'The brothers had always been close but now, I feel their relationship is not so strong. Though I do think they still love each other and will stand by each other in times of trouble. One time when I was young, I remember asking my dad, "If your siblings do something wrong, would you still support them?" And my dad said, "You have to support your family no matter what, even if they do something bad." He always used to say, "Chide them in private but support them in public." Loyalty seems to be the lingering thread between the brothers and only time will tell whether other larger court cases such as the one on the brand will break that final thread or perhaps help make the bond stronger.

The twenty-four-year-old brand battle with the Delhi cousins had already forced the two arms of the family apart, but with Prabhu going to jail, the barons of Delhi felt hard-pressed to immediately publically announce that distance. On 10 February 2010 the owner of the Delhi unit, Manoharlal Agarwal, told the *Telegraph*, 'Yes, we grew up together but his actions cannot be justified. I just feel sad that the Haldiram name has been tainted.'[18] During our interview at his offices in

---

[18] 'Split Is Showing in Bhujia Empire', *Telegraph*, 10 February 2010. http://www.telegraphindia.com/1100210/jsp/calcutta/story_12086326.jsp.

Delhi in June 2015, Manoharlal expressed the same grief he had expressed earlier to the newspaper. He maintained that the sales at the Delhi outlets had not been affected, especially since he and his staff had made it a point to inform all customers that Kolkata and Delhi were two completely separate businesses. Manoharlal mentioned that in June 2005 he had gone to Bikaner to inaugurate a hospital that he had sponsored in order to support his local community. On that very same day, Prabhu had been arrested at the Delhi airport. 'It was funny,' he said, 'a local paper in Bikaner published a story about how one Haldiram owner had just presented Bikaner with a *"bhavya imarat"* (blessed building) followed by a second story about the other Haldiram owner committing a crime—*"Haldiram ke malik giraftar"* (Haldiram owner arrested).' The irony was not lost on anybody.

# PART V

# LEGAL ENTANGLEMENTS

# The Spark That Started the Flame

"This is a twenty-four-year-old war that started in 1991,' said Manoharlal.

The Delhi and Kolkata families have been warring in a Delhi court since 1991 to establish who has the actual right to use the brand names Haldiram Bhujiawala and Haldiram's. While the legal battle only began in the early '90s, the seeds of this enmity were sown a generation before.

Some wounds leave deep scars, especially when they are a result of innumerable tiny cuts that are repeatedly inflicted on the same spot. And scars never really fade away. Over the years, one Agarwal brother hurt another, sometimes unknowingly, and sometimes with malice. Being so close to one another, they knew each other's weaknesses better than anyone else, and exploited them covertly only as family members could. These brothers left behind a legacy of bitterness, anger, and at times hatred, for the generation following close behind. Such a war is not born out of one single incident, rather it is an amalgamation of hurt that set itself upon the Kolkata and Delhi cousins like an unshakeable dark cloud. The fog of pent-up hurt and frustrations created an impenetrable wall, disabling them from being able to view the situation objectively.

The earliest tiny flutters of this massive disgruntlement began between Moolchand and Rameshwarlal when the business was still young and just beginning to move to Kolkata from Bikaner. Perhaps the seeds had been sown even before that, during the innocence of their youthful days together in Bikaner. It was no secret that Moolchand had always been the daddy's boy in spite of having little active interest in the business. All of Moolchand's sons agree that he was his father's biggest follower, always obedient and true. In a way, Haldiram perhaps reciprocated by always being accommodating of his son's lack of interest in the family business and allowing him to slack off unless there was a dire need for him. Perhaps Haldiram's apparently partiality towards Moolchand had built a bank of envy within Rameshwarlal's heart.

It could have also been that Rameshwarlal, being the hardest worker of all his brothers and possibly the most ambitious, had allowed pride and righteousness to come in the way of their relationship. However, it cannot be denied that Haldiram had definitely intended to support Rameshwarlal's ambitions and help him succeed. This is evident in the fact that after setting up the Kolkata arm of the business, he bequeathed his second son all responsibility and ownership of the units there.

One could possibly trace the beginning of the brand battle to intense brotherly rivalry and hurt pride. We saw earlier how affronted Shiv Kishan had felt in Kolkata, especially after some petty accusations and snide remarks levelled by his aunt Kamala Devi. It has been suggested that those very comments were the trigger behind his success in Nagpur, driving him to prove certain relatives wrong. However, that very incident and Shiv Kishan's subsequent rise to prosperity could have also been the pivotal point that had driven Rameshwarlal to do better and better. In some versions of the Mahabharata,

Draupadi laughs at and mocks Duryodhana. Many feel if she had held her laughter, a mammoth war between the two mighty legions could have been avoided. Others believe that Draupadi's mockery was merely the last straw which broke the horse's back. Family members claim that it was Rameshwarlal who wished to become independent of the family business in the early '70s when he approached Moolchand to separate both their entities. However, some claim that it was his wife Kamala Devi who egged him on. Shiv Kishan, during our conversation, had suggested that women, in his view, were the sole reason behind all family issues and enmities. He had said it pointing fingers at nobody in particular, but the strong belief was there to see in his eyes.

Whatever the reasons, one or all of them has led to the brothers fighting their battles in court instead of quietly amongst themselves. Let's trace the story back to the beginning. Ganga Bhishen Agarwal, aka Haldiram began selling bhujia in 1941 in Bikaner and his products became popular by his nickname Haldiram, with most customers. It was by his nickname that his fame grew. The crowds would swarm crying out their demand, 'Haldiramji ki bhujia! Haldiramji ki bhujia!' Haldiram at that time ran a sole proprietorship, since his sons were very young. However, in 1951, he formed a partnership firm with all his three sons, Moolchand, Rameshwarlal and Satyanarayan, trading as Haldiram Bhujiawala under the firm Chandmal Ganga Bishen. People had already begun to associate his products with that brand, demonstrating that this trademark had been acquiring recognition, i.e. a reputation in the market since 1941,' said Aparajita Lath, lawyer, and writer for Spicy IP, a national blog that covers intellectual property issues in India with the aim of bringing about greater transparency.

In 1955, Haldiram, along with Shiv Kishan and Rameshwarlal, went to Kolkata and within a few short years, quickly tasted success. While duty beckoned, so did his home village and original business. Needing to be back with his family in Bikaner, where he belonged, Haldiram bestowed upon his son Rameshwarlal all responsibilities of the Kolkata unit. A couple of years later, Rameshwarlal retired from the partnership business in 1958, according to the case history. The Intellectual Property Appellate Board, however, suggests that Haldiram, out of love for his son, allowed him to use the term 'Haldiram' for his business then, but only in Kolkata.

'At that time, the real business was in Kolkata. That's where the money was made. I mean they made margins of Re 1 or ₹2 per kilo and earned their dues in hard cash. In Bikaner, our business was dependent on traders from outside. A lot of our sales happened on credit and many a time we had to deal with customers who simply refused to pay for our goods. They would make claims such as "the goods didn't arrive in good condition" or "the packaging had given way so we didn't receive everything we ordered", which were all excuses to not pay us. As it is, our margins were very low and with merchants only paying us half of what was owed to us, it made it very hard for us to make a profit some days. Every time you work within parameters of debt, people will find a way to take advantage of you,' said Manoharlal gravely. This was probably true even of the family members, as at the time when Rameshwarlal wanted to cut his losses and separate from his brother and nephews, Moolchand and his sons were in a way indebted to

Kolkata's greater income stream. According to Manoharlal, Moolchand firmly believed that allowing Rameshwarlal to separate would ensure peace between the two brothers and their future families.

With Rameshwarlal having exited, the partnership was now in the name of Haldiram, Satyanarayan, Moolchand and Shivkishan. In 1969, Haldiram dissolved the second partnership and formed another partnership with his son Moolchand, his grandson Shiv Kishan and his daughter-in-law, Kamala Devi, Rameshwarlal's wife who took the place of his third son, Satyanarayan. In 1965, they conceptualized the famous V-shaped 'Haldiram Bhujiawala' logo and registered it as an asset of partnership under a trademark. As per Anurag K. Agarwal, the author of *Business and Intellectual Property: Protect Your Ideas*, 'In December 1972, the said firm applied for registration before the Registrar for trademarks for the registration of the name Haldiram Bhujiawala—Chandmal—Ganga Bhishen Bhujiawala, Bikaner. The registrar of trademarks granted registration with number 285062.' Years after the filing, the trademark was actually registered on 27 January 1981. Within this case, as per the lawyers, the use of the said trademark had been claimed since 1965. In 1974, this group disbanded, breaking the partnership formed just a few years ago.

Legal literature records the big event of 1974 as 'the partnership dissolves'. However, those three words hardly begin to cover the myriad emotions and chaotic dynamics among the family members at the time. In 1968, after being persuaded by his aunt and uncle, Shiv Kishan moved to Nagpur and made a success of his business. He also perhaps came away with a deep sense of pride for his accomplishments as well as resentment for his experience in Kolkata. Family members across the board recount this event as driven by Rameshwarlal's greed. 'In 1968, when our brother Shiv Kishan set up shop in Nagpur, my uncle Rameshwarlal felt a little cheated. While Rameshwarlal had a partnership with the Bikaner branch, he made very little profit out of the partnership, as opposed to the benefits he felt we received from being partners in the Kolkata venture. He approached my father and my father told him that he was content in Bikaner and would be happy to let him fly free. My father declared that Kolkata's business was Rameshwarlal's and that Bikaner's was his. My uncle, at that point, claimed that he didn't care about goodwill and his sole wish was to sell in West Bengal. So he bargained to be allowed to use the logo in West Bengal. "Except West Bengal" he told us to run our business anywhere,' said Manoharlal.

There seems to be a lot of hurt in these memories. An open wound the family has been nursing for many years—rendering them unable to accommodate each other in the present scheme of things. In all probability, Manoharlal and his brothers hold resentment close to their hearts around the memories that their uncle had abandoned them in their time of dire need due to his own voracity and selfishness. It is perhaps impossible to let go of these sentiments, especially once one has gained ground and wants to flaunt one's own power and progress.

So, in 1974, when the partnership dissolved, under the terms of the dissolution deed, Moolchand acquired the right to use the logo and brand name by filing an application with the registrar for trademarks to change the ownership of the trademark from his father's name to his own. According to the case records, Moolchand 'acquires use of trademark across the country except the state of West Bengal'. Kamala Devi was given the right to use the trademark for West Bengal only.

With the partnership no longer holding them together, the brothers went about their business in their different states. Unbeknownst to Moolchand, his sons, Shiv Kishan and Manoharlal, began planning their big move to Delhi; a move definitely within the legal purview of the dissolution deed, as their father now had exclusive trademark rights for the whole country except West Bengal. At the same time, Rameshwarlal and his son, Prabhu Agarwal, secretively applied for registration of the name 'Haldiram Bhujiawala' in Kolkata in 1977. Rameshwarlal's and Prabhu Shankar's intention might have been to protect the right to use the trademark 'Haldiram Bhujiawala' in West Bengal only. But later, in an attempt to capture more, the trademark was registered for the whole of India. According to family members, the Bikaner branch of the Haldiram family were not even aware of such a registration until the start of litigation between the two family lines in December 1991. 'Rameshwarlal registered the same trademark without disclosing that this trademark was already in use. Rameshwarlal was well aware that his father had already applied for registration of the trademark in 1972 since his wife had been a partner in that firm. However, he claimed user status since 1958 just to show that he came into the market before his brother,' said Aparajita Lath. Amazingly, for only this instance the law worked in their favour, and father and son received registration of their trademark number 330375 in 1980 just around the time when two of the Moolchand sons were about to open shop in Delhi. Both the Bikaner and Kolkata businesses were registered to use the trademark 'Haldiram Bhujiawala' at that point.

Just before that, Haldiram had executed his last will dated 3 April 1979, which also echoed the rights conferred by the dissolution deed on the respective parties, i.e. his sons and daughter-in-law, Kamala Devi. In 1980, Haldiram passed away at the age of sixty-two, bequeathing his sons and grandsons with the timeless legacy of bhujia. According to Anurag K. Agarwal, 'His will was later acted upon, giving Moolchand the trademark rights for the entire country except West Bengal. Moolchand died in 1985, leaving behind his four sons—Shiv Kishan, Shiv Ratan, Manoharlal and Madhusudan. All of them had their names recorded as joint proprietors.' However, before Moolchand could peacefully join his father in death, the first of the clashes revolving Delhi as a territory occurred when his sons made the move to start business in the capital.

During my interviews in Kolkata, a curious tale emerged. A close family member who wished to remain anonymous revealed a comedy of errors that occurred in Delhi between '82 and '83. Allegedly, Rameshwarlal got wind of the fact that Manoharlal and Shiv Kishan had planned to open shop in the coveted capital. The grapevine led him to learn that the brothers had already bought property in the heart of Delhi— Chandni Chowk—and that the inauguration was just a few months away. Eagar to jump on the bandwagon and get his show on the capital's streets, Rameshwarlal investigated and discovered a small shop worthy of buying in the same market. He paid an advance and promised to be back in a few weeks to pay the rest. His shop happened to be adjacent to another little bhujiawala's stall.

It is rumoured that the neighbour from the little stall paid Rameshwarlal's soon-to-be landlord ₹3 lakh more than what had been quoted to Rameshwarlal in order to occupy the shop before he could, thereby robbing Rameshwarlal of the opportunity to set up shop at the time. Astonishingly, the little shop belonged to the brand Bikana or Bikanerwala who are today Haldiram's biggest rivals in the traditional foods segment. Shiv Kishan Agarwal confirmed that Bikana belonged to his *nanihal* (wife's mother's side of the family). In this way, as per the relative, Rameshwarlal was thwarted from entering Delhi in the early 1980s.

According to the same family member, it was after this incident that the Kolkata and Delhi families had a verbal agreement that if a family line opens a shop in a particular city, the other family line will not enter that city. They agreed that this would protect the love and trust between the two family lines. It would also ensure that each brother had the freedom and opportunity to grow without restrictions in his city.

Poonam Chand said, 'Rameshwarlal made the verbal agreement and then passed away. It was the children who later created the trouble.'

It seems as if this unique territorial distribution was not forged through purely organic circumstances, but had been a part of Haldiram's protection plan right from the start. Sanctioning one son to work in Kolkata, while ensuring the other son worked in a different territory was Haldiram's strategic vision in action. Even the informal verbal agreement made in the '80s between Moolchand and Rameshwarlal paid homage to the same philosophy of allowing each to grow in independence without encroaching on the other's turf. It was a genius succession plan put in place by Haldiram and then perpetuated by his sons, only to come undone by his grandchildren who threw a spanner in the works. The small flutters of contention that started years ago left a huge impact on the current generation of leaders forcing them to spend their time fighting in courts, rather than focusing on building their empires.

## The Brothers Grim

The age-old grudges of Moolchand and Rameshwarlal were passed down to their sons, leaving them grappling with the bitter seeds of an enmity that had survived beyond their years and their wisdom. Conflicting emotions of loyalty, love, competition and hatred surrounded the cousins, forcing them to view each other as rivals instead of brothers.

The rift between the sons of Rameshwarlal and Moolchand appeared to have grown wider and deeper with each passing year and with each passing court injunction. Even though some cousins diplomatically claim that a bond based on respect still exists, others blatantly reveal the animosity that both sides truly feel for each other. There has been too much hurt, too much that cannot be undone. Ironically, both sides understand the futility of continuing this war and somewhere deep down hope that there might be a way to stop this without realizing that the power to do so lies with them. For now, righteousness leads the charge in this war and its fire still burns bright.

As Mahesh Agarwal so poignantly put, 'Only time will tell whether a side is right or wrong. Everyone fighting the case believes that they are right. In this world, whenever a battle takes place, it is because both parties believe themselves to be right, they believe in their own cause. If even one of them wavers in the conviction of his or her mission, then it won't be a fight anymore, will it?'

Other family members in Kolkata and Bikaner have, over the years, silently formed their opinions on the court battles and subjectively chosen sides, while never outwardly letting on which party they support. Everyone around has gradually gathered that the clash has become pointless, that the brothers simply cannot back down because of bruised egos. Yet, some of them watch the spectacle, secretly revelling in the biggest weakness of the Haldiram family.

During our conversations, Poonam Chand, owner of Bhikharam Chandmal in Kolkata, bitterly said, 'If you have an empty water bottle, you will look around to see how much water the others have in their bottle.' When I couldn't follow, he explained that success was relative and so was power. 'If a brother is weak or makes much less money, the other brother will want to see him less. That's part of the Marwari culture. They (aka Haldiram family) will spend on their neighbours and help them in times of need, but if someone within the family needs help, they will turn a blind eye.'

There is jealousy and bitterness all around. All of their past dealings, including the court case, have enveloped the entire larger family in a dark cloud of misgiving. Trust seems to be hugely lacking, making each party highly possessive of their individual businesses. Their business, money and success have separated them as much as helped them rise in the world.

The actual war began during the darkest period of Prabhu and his brothers' lives. They lost a father and brother all in the space of a few days in 1990. Grief is known to be a potent emotion, but in their case, it came burdened with past hurts and grievances towards the Delhi and Bikaner cousins. Perhaps it was a response to this terrible loss or maybe the deaths were the last straw that broke the camel's back when it came to the silently brewing feud with their cousins. By 1991, Prabhu and his younger brother Ashok had had enough and decided to take action.

When Ravi, their second brother, died in a car accident, they perhaps felt obliged to keep his dream alive. It was, after all, Ravi who had first ventured into Delhi to set up a shop. Yet, while he had worked with Manoharlal and agreed to tailor the brand name to reflect the fact that it was a part of the Kolkata brand, after his death, his brothers refused to be as reasonable. Apparently, in the beginning, the Delhi brothers had been more than willing to accommodate the Kolkata brothers in the city in spite of the agreement within the dissolution deed of 1974, as long as the Kolkata brothers adjusted their brand name to reflect where they were from and differentiate from the Delhi folk, for example, add Kolkata to Haldiram Bhujiawala. However, when the Kolkata cousins were unreasonable and they insisted on entering Delhi using the same brand name of Haldiram's, Manoharlal took the matter to court and the rest is history.

Allegedly, Ashok Agarwal, Prabhu's youngest brother, with consent from his mother, Kamala Devi, planned to open a shop at Arya Samaj Road, Karol Bagh, New Delhi. It was after this move that the Delhi brothers pressed charges. The grapevine reveals multiple reasons for the upcoming court case. Some friends and family members believe that the court case began because the Kolkata brothers had breached the territory plan put in place by Moolchand and Rameshwarlal. Others claimed that Moolchand's sons, still hurt by their uncle's insensitive actions in the past, had felt compelled to evict their Kolkata cousins from the capital. Paradoxically, as it turns out, the issue was definitely a molehill to begin with and could perhaps have been resolved had both parties been more compromising.

According to Anchal Agarwal, the case had everything to do with sanitation and hygiene. 'Ashok chacha moved to Delhi the year that my father, Prabhu chacha, and Ashok chacha divided the Kolkata business [in 1991]. He has been there as far back as I can remember. I remember the shop in Delhi being very disorganized and dirty. I think that is why the Delhi folks filed a court case, as they didn't want their customers to associate Ashok's shop with their brand. They thought the association would sully the brand name,' she said. However, it wasn't an instant reaction. Moolchand's sons claim to have had multiple conversations with their Kolkata cousins, only to be met with firm resistance each time. Their business had also just taken off like a fledgling bird, eager to build its own reputation. With distribution strategies in place, they had just begun to reach a wider population. It was important for them to maintain their image of quality for their customers and with Ashok's shops using the same brand identity, they felt justified in requesting some sort of differentiation in the brand names.

Manoharlal narrates, 'We had only one reason to clash with Ashok. When he started looking into opening a shop in Delhi, we requested them to kindly use a slightly different name. We suggested changing it to "Haldiram Namkeenwala" or maybe "Haldiram Rameshwarlal". We made multiple efforts to work this out with them, but the result was zero. Finally, when we realized that there was no room for negotiation, we took the matter to court at Tees Hazari.' He admits that they would even have been happy to let the Kolkata brothers use 'Haldiram Bhujiawala' as long as they added Kolkata to the name.

Incongruously, as it often is in life, nothing important is ever achieved effortlessly. According to Delhi court records, Moolchand's sons filed a complaint on 10 December 1991. The record says, 'On 10 December 1991 itself an ex parte ad interim injunction was passed against the Appellants herein.' On the twelfth of the same month when Ashok was to inaugurate his shop, the stay order arrived, barring him from doing so. It was then that the mud-slinging began in earnest.

As Manoharlal and his brothers desperately worked to protect their brand name, Ashok and Prabhu aggressively worked towards gaining grounds in Delhi. Although the law had been on the side of the Delhi cousins, the bureaucratic legal system initially worked against them. Through a tiny human error, they lost eight years to the Kolkata brothers, helplessly watching as 'Haldiram Bhujiawala' from Kolkata cannibalized their sales, confused their customers and overall wreaked havoc in the succession system established by their fathers.

In February 1992, the stay order given at the Tees Hazari court was vacated as instead of having the file *transferred* to the high court, the high court official, in an unfortunate error of judgement, ended up *releasing* the case, thereby vacating it. In layman terms, this meant that their stay order became null and void. With the injunction gone, chaos followed. Manoharlal and his brothers then clambered to file a brand new case in the high court and without the injunction in place; Rameshwarlal's sons took advantage of the time gap this lucky break provided as they were no longer required to hold off using the brand name in Delhi for that period.

'Cases involving ₹5 lakh were managed in the lower courts, i.e. courts like the one in Tees Hazari. The minute they exceeded that amount and became even worth ₹6 lakh, they got transferred to a high court. So in this case, the judge used wording such as "I release this case" instead of "I transfer this case", and Ashok's lawyers used this to their benefit. The wording ensured that our existing stay order was nullified,' said Manoharlal.

From 1992–99, Ashok Agarwal ran a couple of outlets in the name of 'Haldiram Bhujiawala', making no effort to distinguish his brand from the existing Delhi brand. In response, pre-empting how difficult this battle was going to be, the Delhi brothers in one single stroke of genius in 1991, changed their name to the now globally renowned 'Haldiram's'. The two sides worked fervently to capture more of the market. Ashok leveraged the Delhi brand's existing loyal customer base to pull them into his outlets, diluting the customer segments between the two brands. Some people claim that the outlets run by the Kolkata brothers—Ashok, supported by his elder brother Prabhu—was not up to the mark and began affecting the brand image and sales of 'Haldiram's'.

Newspaper articles suggest that the earlier Haldiram's outlets were done up in poor taste. A *Times of India* article in 2002 reads: 'The company lacks customer friendly systems and convenience ranks fairly low in their scheme of things— the outlets have no seating arrangement for the elderly, there's insufficient parking space, service is hardly done with a smile.'[19]

---

[19] 'It All Snacks Up', *Economic Times*, 11 December 2002. http://articles. economictimes.indiatimes.com/2002-12-11/news/27339631_1_ brand-valuation-packaging-sweets.

However, family members and close friends of Manoharlal and his son, Pankaj Agarwal claim that these outlets mentioned in the papers had belonged to the Haldiram Bhujiawala brand run by Ashok. This brand dilution and daily melee for sales continued for years even as both parties fervently tried to make headway in the courtrooms.

Manoharlal and his brother Madhusudan ran from pillar to post, trying to comply with the legal requirements to put the injunction back in place. Finally in 1999, the Delhi brothers were able to breathe easy as the high court gave Ashok Agarwal a stay order from 1999–2010. Unable to use the brand name 'Haldiram Bhujiawala' for the next eleven years, Ashok then was legally forced to change the name of his chain outlets to 'Rameshwars'. Rameshwars offered a menu similar to that of Haldiram's with favourites such as chhole bhature and kachoris. In the meantime, Haldiram's was finally free to establish their brand stronger than ever before. The brand grew by strides and began hiring professionals from similar companies to help build a robust empire, while Rameshwars gradually began to pale in comparison, with nothing to differentiate its offer. Seemingly, without the boost that the brand name had given their business initially, Rameshwars found it difficult to truly establish a firm customer base in Delhi, leaving Manoharlal and his sons to dominate the city.

Ominous and unlucky, the freedom zealously fought for, did not last. According to Manoharlal, 'Prabhu and Ashok then appealed to the high court. In 2010, the stay order was vacated and the case was sent back to the lower court in Tees Hazari. At the time the limit for the lower court had increased to ₹25 lakh and our case fell into those parameters. We were back to square one.' He shook his head, frustration seeping from his eyes even now as he recalled the details. However, things had begun to look up for Manoharlal and his brother Madhusudan in Delhi. 'The lower court recognized that Moolchand's family have been trading and have earned goodwill and reputation under the trade name "Haldiram's" for long. Ashok was directed by the lower court to use the trade name "Haldiram Bhujiawala" in analogous font and equal size, along with the V logo, as reflected in Kolkata's family trademark 330375 till the final decision of the IPAB or the disposal of the case. However, it also stipulated that in the meantime, if their trademark was cancelled due to the fact that it had been wrongly filed, they could not use even the Haldiram Bhujiawala brand name.'

The Delhi brothers, Manoharlal and Madhusudan, practised patience, as with the stipulations in place, they believed it was only a matter of time before the tide turned in their favour. The IPAB finally resolved this issue in 2013 by ordering the removal of the trademark registration made in favour of Kolkata in 1980. According to Aparajita Lath, 'The board held that Mr Rameshwarlal was only a permitted user and could not be the proprietor of the said mark . . . it was also noted that Mr Rameshwarlal had knowledge of the fact that it was Mr Bishen [Haldiram] who had first coined the name "Haldiram Bhujiawala". Therefore, Mr Rameshwarlal cannot claim to be the inventor and adopter himself . . . On the point of the date of use, the board observed that the date mentioned was based on a false statement, as the respondents were aware of Mr Bishen's mark, which was identical, claiming use since 1965.'

With the trademark denied to the Kolkata business, the Delhi firm could now conduct business, fearless of any cannibalism. However, Manoharlal claims that in spite of the IPAB order, Ashok is to this date running branches under the name of 'Haldiram Bhujiawala' in Delhi.

In 2014, Prabhu Agarwal started using the brand name 'Haldiram Prabhuji's', which was not yet registered, when the IPAB, Chennai, cancelled their registered trademark Haldiram Bhujiawala with the V logo (numbered 330375) in April 2013.

When I questioned Prabhu, he refused to comment on the matter, claiming that his Delhi and Nagpur brothers will always speak the truth and tell no lies. He seemed to hold that stance throughout the interview in a bid to perhaps hold on to his dignity or perchance as a belated display of camaraderie with his Delhi cousins.

I pushed a little harder, asking him about his next steps now that they had lost the court case. Finally, curt and ruffled, he said, 'If Shiv Kishan or Manoharlal have said anything about the case, they shouldn't have. This is a family matter.' Challenge sparked briefly in his eyes before he continued, 'In India there are lower courts, high courts and a Supreme Court. The final decision has not yet been made. If I have lost the case, then this is not the final defeat. This battle has been going on for twenty years and it might go on for twenty more.' He refused to say anything further on the matter. In spite of multiple phone calls, his brother, Ashok Agarwal, was unavailable for comments.

Mahesh, however, shared his sentiments. 'Rameshwarlal was the first user since 1958. Moolchandji's registration was done in 1965 as they started using the trademark later, and the trademark depends on prior use. The partnership firm formed in 1974 said that all partners could use the trademark everywhere except West Bengal. However, after Haldiramji and Moolchandji passed away, his sons made a dissolution deed stating that the trademark had been first used by them, which we feel is a fraud.'

Anchal's view was surprisingly inconsistent with her side of the family, especially on the subject of why the war started in the first place. 'I don't know much about the case. But if the Delhi guys were allowing us to keep our Kolkata brand name with the simple change of adding Kolkata to the logo, I think it was fair. But, I didn't know that.'

By the sound of it, it seems like neither party is willing to meet midway and that the court case will probably go on for years to come. Allegedly, lakhs and lakhs of rupees have been spent on sustaining the case. According to Poonam Chand, 'Every month Manohar comes to attend court sessions in Kolkata. It costs them ₹2 lakh per date just in terms of lawyer fees, let alone flights and hotel charges.' The case has exhausted not just the main players, but also bystanders. Both Manoharlal's son Pankaj Agarwal and nephew Ashish Agarwal (Madhusudan's son) held that the court case had been a huge strain on the family and the business. Both insisted that if they could have spent all that energy towards strategically building the business, they would probably be on a much higher plane today. The scions believe that the last twenty-four years have been a waste, but as they put it, "brands matter, especially our own".

While newspaper reports claim that the family meets every monsoon in Bikaner, the family members readily admit that the love between the family lines of Moolchand and Rameshwarlal has diminished. Shiv Kishan said, 'Our bonds are broken now.

I guess if we ever bump into each other and Prabhu greets me, I will definitely greet him back politely, but that feeling has been lost.' Prabhu, on the other hand, seemed to nurse a delusion that everything was fine between them and this animosity only extended to the professional sphere, and not to their family lives. He kept suggesting that the lines of communication between the two had always been open and that what bonded the cousins were their common goals of forever protecting the brand and the quality of the products.

Compelled to act on what they each believed to be injustices, they felt their hands forced into taking extreme measures for supposed vengeance. They have been fighting in the courts for over two decades, yet, neither party is willing to withdraw or compromise even today. The devastation of this war has been immeasurable in terms of money and resources wasted and emotions drained. Exhausted and desperate for it to end, the two sides are still unable to call a truce and move on from this fight. The fight has, in a way, become a part of their existence; a habit so deeply ingrained that they find it almost impossible to let go of it.

In spite of this ongoing battle, each business has independently stretched the limits of their regions and succeeded in finding new avenues of success. Even while they are bound by territorial agreements nationally, together they export their goods to over sixty countries internationally, making them India's largest indigenous processed food company. As the current owners start looking to the baton over to their sons, it remains to be seen how the businesses will survive the brand battle and intense competition in the market.

# PART VI

# FINAL PACES

## Steps and Strides

Sitting in Dr Tyagi's third floor corporate office in Delhi in June 2015, I finally allowed the overwhelming tingle of awe to seep in. This four-storeyed sturdy glass-and-steel building captured everything that the global corporate offices of one of India's super brand should look like. Dr Tyagi was at home in his window suite even while wearing a full suit and tie in the heat of the Delhi summer. The air conditioning hummed a familiar beat while I waited for him to divulge his organization's latest secrets. Manoharlal spent most of his time on the fourth floor of this building, with an almost prescient aura in all dealings within the building and the business. The bottom two floors were filled with workers and the occasional sound of a drill broke through my reverie. Research and development and training departments were to be set up down there alongside a tasting laboratory. The building spoke of opulence and prestige. It was a long way to come from a simple hovel in a small town in Rajasthan.

Dr Tyagi had joined Haldiram's as the president and CEO of the company in 2006 from Uncle Chips. Today, he is executive director, overlooking production, manufacturing, sales, marketing and innovation. That's an enormous portfolio for one person to be looking after. So why did he move to a traditionally run, family-owned Indian food brand? His motivation emanated from early scintillating conversations with the chief managing director, Manoharlal Agarwal, whom he called a 'brand creator, a great visionary and an unparalleled initiator'.

Dr Tyagi was one of the first outsiders to join Haldiram and since he was hired; the crew has only grown grander. As the number of non-family members has risen among the ranks, so has the attempt to professionalize the business, automate it and streamline processes to make them more efficient. This, in turn, has thrown up several challenges, forcing the family to adapt and firefight, while laying down a new constitution for the future.

At the time when Dr Tyagi had joined the business, there were no middle layers of management in the company. The karigars were in direct contact with the management (owners) and were accustomed to this strong relationship. Newcomers like Dr Tyagi have struggled to earn the respect of the workers and establish their authority in the hierarchy of things. 'The karigars are people from an earlier era when there was no line of command between them and us. They find it difficult to accept new professionals due to psychological reasons. It is important that the professionals, in turn, understand our company culture and make double the effort to build a rapport with these men who form the foundation of our business,' said Pankaj Agarwal. While cultural reasons play a role, other factors such as education levels, competition and change are key to understanding the strife between these two sets of employees within the organization.

'Suppose I hire someone from Amul, another person from PepsiCo, and a third from Britannia, to join our sales team— each person hired today has to be technically qualified from one of the top universities so that they can help elevate the professionalism in the organization. When we try to fit these educated individuals among the ranks, there will not only be a difference in salaries but also in the way tasks are approached, as the new employees are modern and systems-oriented,' said Dr Tyagi.

Hiring and building the team has been a long-drawn-out process. Dr Tyagi started his tenure at Haldiram's by improving the structure of the sales organization within the company. Although originally the company viewed North India as one region, Dr Tyagi, with support from the management team streamlined sales into four regions in the North. With territories divided, an extensive performance management system was put in place with goals established in the form of percentages of market shares that trickled down to the most junior salesperson on the teams. The entire organization was re-valuated and salespeople were allotted to a region based on the area, the potential of the region and the potential of the outlets in the region. Sales expenditure is currently 1 per cent of the entire sales, and in line with the annual operating margin goals. This would include salaries, commissions and bonuses for the deployed sales force. Dr Tyagi runs a tight ship under the guidance of Manoharlal. 'I did not try to achieve this instantly! One salesperson at a time was added to the team, giving the existing employees a chance to adjust to the inevitable changes. The CMD has always been supportive and understood the need for modernizing the processes. Both father and son want the organization to be professional and have focused their energies towards achieving that goal,' he said.

Similar initiatives across the organization and all its departments demonstrate the Moolchand family's commitment to this change. While family members, including Manoharlal Agarwal, Madhusudan Agarwal and their sons, and karigars who have worked for the family for years still grossly outnumber non-family professionals, the company has slowly but surely started the journey towards professionalizing its culture. The opportunities to make an impact on the business are tremendous, and professionals have taken up this mantle with a passion. Sumon Chatterjee, senior manager for supply chain and HR at Haldiram's, comments on the diversity of his role, saying that even though the company is already a hugely established business, employees like him have the opportunity to add diverse skills to their resumes and help instigate change that will surely make a difference in the years to come.

According to Sumon, while relationships are Haldiram's greatest strength, they also need to be reviewed and assessed for their value as time goes on. 'We have key suppliers that the family has worked with since they started out in Delhi. For example, we have only one supplier for dry fruits.' His eyes widened to emphasize the bizarreness of that fact. 'We don't have any backups for that category of raw materials and the family is hesitant to drive that change. Even if costs are a bit high, it is difficult for them to break these relationships for commercial reasons. It is commendable that they respect these ties. I mean, this is why they have such a loyal network of suppliers and distributors, but in a modern business, it is also important to never compromise on time and efficiency, and vetting suppliers plays a major role in that process,' he said.

Most professionals within the Haldiram's team admitted that while they are developing processes within the company and enhancing existing norms, it has also been a remarkable learning experience for them to grow with the family. Haldiram's is at the delicate cusp of emerging as a strong player in the national and global processed foods industry. There are immense opportunities for professionals to be harbingers of this change and drive the company towards growth and success.

The company's own heritage proves to be a very sturdy foundation for this growth. Only rarely can companies boast of multiple generations of the same family having worked for them. The Haldiram family have supported their community through the ages by inviting workers from their hometown to work with them when they moved to other big cities, and Babu Singh is one such example. Babu Singh's father had worked with the family for forty years, before the son himself began working with them. Babu Singh moved from Bikaner to Delhi, dedicating himself to the 'family' business, as he endearingly puts it. He started off with a monthly salary of ₹300 in 1985 and today earns ₹72,000 a month as the manager of the Chandni Chowk outlet. Both his children study in Birla's Pilani school. Loyalty and hard work are definitely valued by the family in Delhi. 'All my learning in life comes from them. The managing director, Manoharlal Agarwal, is also our guru. They have demonstrated no ego over the years. They listen to all ideas, no matter whom they come from. That is the greatest part of working with them,' he said.

When asked what he thought about change and whether the family was struggling with change in terms of the workforce, Babu vehemently disagreed. 'You see that shop in front ours?' I noticed a small shuttered-down shop across the street. 'Yes, that one,' he confirmed. 'That shop is 200 years old. It could have been successful even today, but the owner only ever made and sold one product through his entire career—desi ghee. He never diversified. Even today when health trends have hit our market, he didn't evolve and he had to shut down.' Babu explained how in his mind, Haldiram's had always tried to stay ahead of the curve, with products that addressed every changing customer need. He had complete faith that this switch to professionalism, while not easy, could be accomplished. For an employee that was hardly educated beyond a few years in school, Babu has displayed inherent business acumen, which he claims he learnt from the Agarwal family.

Even while Delhi is moving towards a more professional work environment, Nagpur and Kolkata struggle to put trust beyond their immediate family and friends. Shiv Kishan explained, 'The quality of professionals here is very low. Being a small town, Nagpur does not attract or retain talent. Most of those who are highly educated, seek greener pastures in Delhi or even abroad and the rest are not of a calibre that will impact our business.' Trust plays a huge role here as both Shiv Kishan and Prabhu Shankar rely on friends to fill trusted positions. For example, Shiv Kishan's personal secretary is the daughter of a supplier and close confidant while Prabhu's factory managers are sons of long-time business associates. They hold the reins to their business close to their chest and are not even thinking about professionalizing. 'There are too many internal loose ends to tie up before we invite outsiders into the business,' said Shiv Kishan, highlighting that there were miles to go before they could compete with their Delhi siblings.

Simultaneously, having hired more people, Haldiram's in Delhi was putting every resource it possibly could into training them and bringing them up to speed. Workers in the restaurants come with multiple challenges such as an almost non-existent knowledge of the business, lack of communication skills and low confidence. The training cell in the corporate offices in Noida focuses on helping these workers deliver a consistent message which is true to their brand through verbal and non-verbal communication.

Although Haldiram's has been focused on modernizing the equipment in their factories over the years and have achieved a high level of hygiene and automation, they are yet to be labelled 'advanced' in another major operational area. 'The second challenge is the lack of processes itself,' said Pankaj Agarwal. 'There isn't enough documentation in our processes. A lot depends on the people currently. For instance, if we bring in a fresher, train him and expect him to make dosa for customers, it will be a huge challenge for him as he won't know what temperature he has to keep the girdle plate on for the perfect product.' He demonstrated a keen sensitivity to the challenges of the workforce and was driven by the desire to help facilitate them, which was a refreshing perspective to come across.

The company is currently on overdrive to develop and establish processes, right from ordering and receiving raw material to delivering the final product to the customer. The focus on standardization will help the organization prepare itself for further expansion by setting up processes that can easily be replicated at newer outlets and factories, thereby giving them an edge over their many competitors. In spite of this continuous bid to improve, Haldiram's has come a long way from when it first started out in the capital.

Pankaj recalls, 'When in school, my brothers, cousins and I would visit the shop and factory in Chandni Chowk almost daily.

In those days, everything was very discouraging. Those times were different . . . the conditions were different. Safety for our workers was low, there would be fire blazing from the pits and people working in dangerous conditions. I wasn't interested in joining the business until I finished my MBA. Post-Switzerland, it was the tremendous opportunity to bring about change and impact the business that motivated me. The challenges of running a family business that had once seemed daunting, today feels like a ladder for self-accomplishment. Every day we learn something new and every day I feel like something has been achieved.'

When asked to exemplify some of his biggest contributions to the business, he humbly said, 'I have no achievements to talk of. Nothing that will make you stop and say "aha". All my work has simply been organic.' It seemed Pankaj carried a chip on his shoulder, where he believed that one could only be seen as an achiever if one had started something from the ground up, an example of working with a father with a brilliant history in entrepreneurship. Pankaj looked up to his father throughout his career and even today puts him on a pedestal. His drive to grow the business comes from wanting to do Manoharlal proud.

He has many plans for the immediate future—from imploding the market with the choicest range of frozen products to building an e-commerce platform for the company, leveraging another channel for growth. With Indians internationally buying the Haldiram's brand, Pankaj believes that frozen foods would be the best product to reach the global customer. 'Having looked at the competitors' products, I believe there are also several synergies that we can leverage with our existing product. I mean we already make fantastic chhole; all we have to work on is technology and adjusting the recipe to ensure that it is perfect for frozen conditions.' In spite of sky-high ambitions, they face immense challenges as they compete with established brands in the US and other countries such as Deep Foods that have strong distribution and warehousing resources in these markets. Nonetheless, having conducted market research and spoken to several Indians abroad, he feels fairly confident that the Haldiram's brand, due to its familiarity and visibility, will quickly gain ground, especially with the millennials.

Another pet project is launching a factory in the UK. Father and son together bought the plant five years ago but several concerns on the home front diverted their attention. Pankaj hopes to have established this factory by 2020. 'The whole idea is to set up a facility outside India for dairy products because of the challenge we face in exporting,' he said. Apparently, any dairy product made in India, even by companies such as Nestle', is not fit to be exported to the West. This is because the standard of raw milk in the western countries is not even achieved post-pasteurization in India due to the processes and lack of education on animal feed and hygiene. 'In the US, we get our main volume through ethnic stores; however, the UK is a huge market for us. A large number of mainstream grocery stores such as Waitrose, Tesco, etc. stock our products, and the sales are great! We are looking forward to releasing products such as tinned rasgullas and gulab jamuns.' This will be a huge victory for Haldiram's since at the moment they are selling packaged snacks and sweet boxes. The tinned sweets will reach a wider clientele looking for instant dessert in bite-size packages. It also has a longer shelf life.

Aspirations towards international expansion are accompanied by a desire to be available on the exploding new platform of mobile apps on home ground in Delhi. Multiple new apps have formed a brand new industry in India's largest cities, providing deliveries of food to customers who place orders on their laptops, tablets and mobile phones. Companies such as Zomato and Food Panda have revolutionized the concept of takeout by offering such services to mobile-savvy professionals at their fingertips. The young businessman, Pankaj, wants to take advantage of Haldiram's already excellent food lines to successfully serve online customers. 'At the moment, we are just thinking logistics. Gurgaon seems like the best place to test out a pilot as the demographics include a young and busy professional group of people. We're excited about the idea of being able to offer customers food delivery services via mobile apps, though at the moment our biggest concern is identifying the most efficient supply chain model to support this possible new development. We will, of course, start a whole new brand for the platform as people have certain expectations of our existing brand and might not be too pleased to see a menu with, say, no chhole bhature.' He wants to keep the customers guessing about the exact nature of the new brand and its future product lines.

Customers have always been the centre of everything at all of the Haldiram brands. Following the latest health trends, all business units are focusing on strengthening their baked goods product lines and responding to the healthy eating trends with traditional versions of low-fat snacks. To this end, hygiene and quality are of even greater importance than ever before. Even as the three units in Bikaner, Nagpur and Kolkata admit that Delhi is the most automated of them all, they struggle to modernize their facilities and improve the conditions of their workers. There is a thrust on safety, clean hands, face masks to reduce contamination, and sanitization in the day-to-day processes at these businesses, setting them apart from most other Indian food brands in the market.

The various business units are also employing innovative and smarter methods to reduce costs and also lower their carbon footprints. In Nagpur, Shiv Kishan reconfigured his factory at Gumthala to be powered by solar energy. 'It cost us ₹6 crore to set up the solar plant. While we spent a lot of money on it, it helps keep the environment clean; at the same time we save a lot of money in terms of electricity bills that we no longer have to pay.' The Nagpur branch took advantage of the government subsidies to set up their cost-saving solar plant; however, it takes a forward-looking approach to put in a lot of money upfront for long-term benefits. Prabhu in Kolkata did a one-up on Nagpur. He put his waste material to work for him by setting up a thermal heat exchanger. The machine converts the husk of rice into energy. Prabhu claims, 'Not only will production go up by 300 per cent, but I'm estimating that each person's time will be saved by one hour. In this plant, we have approximately 100 workers and so that's 100 hours saved per day. Also, regular energy costs ₹100 and this costs ₹40, leading to 60 per cent savings.'

Succeeding at business has been a top priority for each of these men; however, they have also found innovative ways in which to contribute to society. All the CSR ventures have stemmed from their Marwari intuition, ensuring that they made zero losses, if not some profits. Manoharlal set up a hospital in Bikaner, followed by Prabhu's brothers who did the same in Kolkata. In 2010, Manoharlal set up a cardiovascular hospital named Haldiram Moolchand, and donated it to the

Rajasthan government. Moolchand had passed away due to heart afflictions, and it is to support the cause of a healthy heart that Manoharlal felt compelled to start this initiative. Having spoken to friends and family, all of whom tout Manoharlal to be a very generous and charitable soul, it came to light that a couple of years ago, he had set up a school in Noida—Gyaanshree, which has not yet broken even. The idea is to develop an education system that values holistic learning, encouraging children to learn yoga, sports and music alongside academics so as to graduate as independent, confident individuals. The school follows global standards of pedagogical practices to help create a system that is more measurable, but at the same time offers students 'effortless and meaningful learning'. Fees and admission are subsidized on a case-by-case basis and already the school has been ranked number one by the Times School Survey of 2015.

## The Long View

Sitting in a black leather chair in the impressive boardroom with its extensive woodwork at his office in Noida, Pankaj looked pensively at the gigantic Ganesha statue claiming the spotlight in the room. The forty-something heir to the Delhi enterprise weighed his words carefully before responding to my question, 'What are your dreams for this business?'

As he stared into the distance lost in thought, I wondered if he had forgotten I was in the room. He then looked up at me, smiled apologetically and answered in his characteristic soft voice: 'I want us to become a world-class organization. I want Haldiram's to be the top preferred employer in the food industry in India. Mostly, I want to help set up a model within family-owned businesses in a way that people will look up to us and wish that their family businesses had a structure such as ours.'

Pankaj raved about American and European family businesses such as Johnson & Johnson, De'Longhi, Lego and the Hermes Group, that have survived generations to form a successful business culture and credo which are followed by thousands of employees worldwide. Citing the study by Harvard that 70 per cent of family businesses do not survive past the third generation, he hopes that his brothers and uncles together will be able to develop and implement a succession plan that will protect their legacy for generations to come. 'I spoke to my father about this, and years ago we tried to pursue a path with a formalized succession plan. My uncles in Nagpur and Bikaner were included and a consultant from Tamil Nadu helped take us through the paces to what a clear constitution would look like. However, it fizzled out and everybody lost interest.' He hopes that they can pick up where they left off sooner rather than later.

Perhaps there is now a need to have these discussions at the unit level, given how each brother is managing his business units independently. Delhi is the largest at approximately ₹3000 crore annual revenues, while Nagpur (₹2000 crore) and Bikaner (the Bikaji brand, ₹1500 crore) compete for the second and third spots. Family members wonder whether the Delhi branch's success is due to the ingenuity of their leaders or whether it is luck—the luck of having bagged the capital as their territory. Shiv Kishan admitted that his sons often asked him why he gave up Delhi, lamenting that they could've had a far better future in the capital city. However, he always wisely told them, 'We have plenty of demand here in Nagpur. Let's set up twenty more outlets here first and then we can talk.'

The family business brings with it multiple advantages as well as challenges. Most members argued that the family itself is the greatest benefit they had. It meant working with people that one could trust and rely on to pool resources and expand. 'There is a lot of flexibility and people do not judge you.' It also enables members to be autonomous and make decisions based on their intuition without having to follow a long chain of command. However, it also increases the risk of trust issues and the desire to covet. It is, therefore, really important to establish a succession plan to ensure there is no confusion about expectations, responsibilities and benefits of being a part of the business.

Companies like J&J have set up a credo that identifies the qualifications members should have. They also have a clearly laid-out process in terms of the criteria for successfully growing within the business. 'The whole process of starting at a particular position, learning your way up and then making it to a position where you have the authority to make decisions is missing. Currently, when one of us joins the business, they join as part of the management team of directors, whether or not they are capable of performing the job required. This puts the business at risk and is perhaps the most pertinent reason why family businesses fail,' said Pankaj.

Succession planning is the key to their future success as also understanding the role of family members in the business. Ashish Agarwal recalls how he had struggled to play 'boss' right after passing out of management school. 'This business was built on the foundation of strong relationships. I came in the door, eager to prove myself and ended up alienating several of our key contractors and workers simply because I was too authoritative for them. Instead of seeking to first understand, I sought to change. That was the first lesson for the boss's son and nephew.' At a young age, the heirs are given the responsibility of thousands of crores of rupees, yet there is no structure, documentation or process in place to help initiate them into the ways of the business. The young padawans learn as they go, sometimes making huge mistakes and at other times achieving minor wins. Without a system in place, they lack discipline and organization. Arriving late for meetings, making suppliers wait for hours to catch up with them, coming to work at no fixed times are some of the lapses and luxuries that come with being a part of a family business.

Passions run high and each of them loves the business more than anything else. However, being born with a silver spoon, they find it hard to stick to professional habits. The awareness and desire for change is there, and slowly but surely the organization is moving towards more global standards or work quality.

However, this 'malik ka beta/beti' tag is as much a stigma as a badge of honour for them. These heirs come with the burden of being associated with the family brand. Anchal Agarwal explains how she is very reserved about the family business in her academic circles since with the name come the scandals, the court drama, and the judgement that she was born in a rich family and did not have to work a day in her life. The exposure of studying abroad and in other cities in India, helped each of them admire, appreciate and accept the other classes of society, such as those working in 'service', as they put it, and learn that to modernize, they will have to adapt and change their ways to accommodate the global working culture.

Moving towards a strong succession plan is important, but the family also needs to learn how to be a family business without having to share the same physical space. Pankaj, in a bid to live out his independence, moved out of the family bungalow at J-15, Hauz Khas Enclave, to live separately with his wife and daughters. 'It was extremely difficult. Nobody in our family has done this, at least not since Haldiramji and it wasn't an amicable move for him. One needs to learn to be mature and move on to maintain the love as opposed to live in the same space and stop talking to one another. This change is inevitable.' His cousin Ashish supports his move by commenting on how open lines of communication were more important than living under one roof. This is a huge transformation for the family, but they seem to be taking this adjustment, like all the others, in their stride. Currently, Manoharlal, his wife and two sons and families as well as Madhusudan's family of four sons and their wives live in the family bungalow. Pankaj is the only one who seems to have struck out by himself. While the family is definitely growing and evolving with the times, the business is still purely run by the men. Pankaj gently admits that his wife had never been involved in the business and when it came to his daughters, it seemed to be a novel idea to him that someday they might want to be a part of the business.

Growth occupies Pankaj's mind space almost all the time. He dreams of taking the business to new planes of success but, like all entrepreneurs, accedes that certain limitations will always be present. 'We have to find a way to work around them, don't we?' he asked me with a mischievous twinkle in his eyes. 'An IPO is almost impossible for us. Unfortunately, the way the brands are divided, it will be very confusing for both our customers and our stakeholders. The internal structure is also not geared towards it.' The business is following an ambitious trajectory to progress nonetheless, focusing on projects with greater return on investment, such as distribution of new product lines in India and abroad. Acquisitions play a role as the company embraces the limitations of its brands and reach. For instance, the recent acquisition of Yumkeen from Uncle Chips is one such example. 'The brand was lying idle, making this first one a very easy acquisition for us. We bought only the trademark, not facilities or machinery, but this will enable us to reach a customer segment that Haldiram's could never before,' added Pankaj. Yumkeen will be a lower-priced brand that focuses on the lower-middle-class populace, filling the gap that Haldiram's, with its value for money, quality image couldn't.

In spite of the 'sky is the limit' growth plans, challenges lurk at every corner. Following the hacking of the Maggi brand, Haldiram's was thrown into the same notorious limelight. The FDA came down upon the brand and sent back some of their consignments. For the nation, it was just another case of violation. For the family, the incident was a nightmare. 'It was standard procedure. The FDA conducts regular checks on consignments and if they find something that doesn't sit within their parameters, they serve a notice, conduct lab tests, and if the product isn't up to their standards, they ask you to destroy that batch. Because of the Maggi episode, suddenly there was a lot of publicity about the issue. However, we were exporting before that episode, we exported during the episode and we continue to export after,' said Pankaj.

Apparently, sanitization and quality of raw materials is an issue most Indian companies face due to the conditions of production in the country. In Haldiram's case, spices turned out to be the major source of contamination. Ever since that incident, they have come down hard on their suppliers, made processes even more stringent and are focused on delivering the highest quality of goods. But all said, the incident did affect their sales for a short period.

'It was quite nerve-wracking because while our exports were not affected, there were major repercussions. Maggi was the hot news of the day and suddenly after the media attention a lot of agencies in India became active and began pulling up our products. Maggi had become zero overnight. Such a big, powerful brand simply disappeared into the night and our biggest worry was that if something like that happened to us, what would we do? Nestlé has multiple brands under its umbrella; however, all we have is our family legacy of Haldiram's. It was frightful,' said Pankaj.

His impassioned tone gave a quick peek into the vulnerability the family felt during the situation with the FDA. It also gave insights into how much the business means to the family. It is all they have ever known. 'It's a part of my identity. I'm from a family business. I have never once stopped to examine that statement, but it has long since become a part of my introduction to people I meet for the first time,' said Anchal Agarwal.

Prabhu, in his own words, described the business as the road to nirvana. '*Tripti ka saadhan*,' he called it. He tried explaining it as the most beautiful responsibility in the world, even as he stuttered like a father describing fatherhood for the very first time. 'Our customers love the brand. It is my greatest honour to be able to satisfy them on a daily basis. It's an ambition that holds a great meaning to me.'

Each of them is so involved in the daily ins and outs of the business that there is nothing else they think about. According to Pankaj, it is difficult to even come up with a barely viable business idea outside the food industry. 'This is all we know. This space is the only space that seems to get our creative juices flowing. We achieve our purpose through the business.'

While each line of siblings loves the brand in similar ways, it is unfortunate that they continue to fight over their branding rights and their territories. Even whilst being harassed by family strife, they seek innovative technologies and processes to improve their business and strive to make a better impact on the communities around them. They have built hospitals and schools and spent lakhs of rupees on sustainable energy plants, indirectly helping the country become a better place. Whether these territorial separations have helped them succeed or held them back, we might never know. However, we do know and understand our deep love for bhujia in whichever part of the world we might be.

'What drives you?' I finally asked Pankaj Agarwal while we sipped our cups of steaming hot masala chai. He replied with enthusiastic idealism, 'Passion. If you are passionate about what you do, ideas and inspiration will bloom in your mind, every second of every day. But if that passion fades, you will become a misfit, demotivated and lost. I ask myself if I'm passionate about Haldiram's every day, and the answer is always *yes*.'

# ACKNOWLEDGEMENTS

Since a thank you only takes a moment . . .

To my husband and best friend, Aditya, without whose unwavering belief and encouragement, I would never have finished this book, achieved this dream.

To my parents, for their unconditional love, and childlike excitement over all my achievements.

To my friend, mentor and fellow author, Nikhil Inamdar, for believing in me and setting me on my journey.

To my editor, Radhika Marwah, for her enthusiasm, diligence and love for the story.

Finally, to the people without whom this book would not have been possible—each and every member of the Haldiram family who took the time out to share their personal stories with me.